W9-CEW-680

Summer Doorways

Books by W. S. Merwin

POEMS

Present Company
Migration: New & Selected Poems
The Pupil
The River Sound
The Folding Cliffs
The Vixen
Travels
The Rain in the Trees
Opening the Hand
Finding the Islands
The Compass Flower
The First Four Books of Poems
Writings to an Unfinished Accompaniment
The Carrier of Ladders
The Lice
The Moving Target
The Drunk in the Furnace
Green with Beasts
The Dancing Bears
A Mask for Janus

PROSE

The Ends of the Earth
The Mays of Ventadorn
The Lost Upland
Unframed Originals
Regions of Memory
Houses and Travellers
The Miner's Pale Children

TRANSLATIONS

Sir Gawain and the Green Knight
Dante's Purgatorio
East Window: The Asian Translations
From the Spanish Morning
Four French Plays
Vertical Poetry (Poems by Roberto Juarroz)
Pieces of Shadow: Selected Poems of Jaime Sabines
Selected Translations 1968–1978
Osip Mandelstam, Selected Poems (with Clarence Brown)
Asian Figures
Transparence of the World (Poems by Jean Follain)
Voices (Poems by Antonio Porchia)
Products of the Perfected Civilization (Selected Writings of Chamfort)
Twenty Love Poems and a Song of Despair (Poems by Pablo Neruda)
Selected Translations 1948–1968
The Song of Roland
Lazarillo de Tormes
Spanish Ballads
The Satires of Persius
The Poem of the Cid

Summer Doorways

A MEMOIR

W. S. MERWIN

Shoemaker Hoard

Library of Congress Cataloging-in-Publication Data
Merwin, W. S. (William Stanley), 1927–
Summer doorways : a memoir / W. S. Merwin
p. cm.
HARDCOVER: ISBN (10): 1-59376-072-8 (ALK. PAPER), ISBN (13): 978-1-59376-072-4
PAPERBACK: ISBN (10): 1-59376-118-X, ISBN (13): 978-1-59376-118-9
1. Merwin, W. S. (William Stanley), 1927—Childhood and youth.
2. Merwin, W. S. (William Stanley), 1927—Travel—Europe.
3. Poets, American—20th century—Biography. 4. Europe—
Description and travel. 5. Americans—Europe—Biography.
I. Title.
PS3563.E75Z474 2005
811'.54—dc22   2005010494

Text design by David Bullen
Printed in the United States of America by Malloy

 Shoemaker & Hoard
An Imprint of Avalon Publishing Group, Inc.
1400 65th Street, Suite 250
AVALON
publishing group incorporated
Emeryville, CA 94608
Distributed by Publishers Group West
10 9 8 7 6 5 4 3 2 1

To

Galway Kinnell and

Edmund Keeley

Summer Doorways

1

A summer descends to us from earlier years, heir to ancestors it never knew. The summer I was twenty-one I sailed for Europe. I left from New York, the city where I had been born, though I had not grown up there. Except for a walk with my parents across the international bridge at Niagara Falls, to step on the soil of Canada when I was, I think, eight, it was the first time I had been out of the country.

Travel from America to Europe became a commonplace, an ordinary commodity, some time ago, but when I first went such departure was still surrounded with an atmosphere of adventure and improvisation, and my youth and inexperience and all but complete lack of money heightened that vertiginous sensation. So did the fact that we went by sea, which took days, rather than a few hours by air.

Four of us were to be travelling together on the boat. At that age I was already married. That was a rash, unconsidered arrangement, not destined to last, and indeed already coming undone, but my wife, Dorothy, was with me. We planned to meet the other two who would be with us at the boat. One of them was Peter Stuyvesant, twelve years old, whom I had tutored the summer before, and the other was a school friend of Peter's named Andrew, who was coming along so that Peter would have company his own age.

It was early July and very hot. The last week or so had been a kind of interregnum, a time of packing and packing up, of goodbyes and outings. Dorothy's sister's boyfriend had a new Studebaker convertible with a radiator ornament like a small airplane, and we dreamed up reasons for trips from the boyfriend's house in Princeton, to the Jersey shore, Dorothy's parents' tiny old house beside the derelict canal west of the Delaware in Morrisville, Pennsylvania, and New York. We spent the last day and night in Manhattan, in a minute apartment that had been lent to Dorothy's sister, in midtown on the East Side. It was long before the days of air-conditioning. The windows were all open to the New York summer night, and Dorothy's sister and a friend of hers who was also spending the night there on a couch complained knowledgeably and at length about how high rents had become in New York. Someone they knew had just taken an apartment nearby, nothing but a studio with a kitchen and bathroom and balcony, and it was costing their friend *ninety* dollars a month.

The next morning there were traffic problems in midtown. The whole of that part of New York was tied up by a huge parade for Douglas MacArthur down Fifth Avenue. The radios were blaring commentaries on it. We heard every word through the open windows. Pundits were speculating about the possibility of his running for president. Just before we were scheduled to leave, an assistant editor from the *Hudson Review* arrived at the apartment bringing me the page proofs of a review I had written for the magazine, for me to correct on the voyage and send back. It was a piece about Lord Acton and Jacob Burckhardt, about historians, about history. What did I know about history? But the delivery of page proofs at that moment made me feel, as we inched through the jammed side streets, heading for our wharf across the East River, that I was really a writer.

✳　✳　✳

Our passage had been booked on the *Nyhorn,* a Norwegian freighter registered in Panama, as I was told by one of the crew who helped with the trunks, or in Liberia, as I was informed definitively a bit later by the plump, bustling, officious young man who was the steward assigned to look after the few passengers, whose cabins and dining and sitting rooms were under the bridge.

The steward was right. It was the Liberian flag we saw on the flagstaff that first morning at sea. After we had watched the closing of the hatches and the final readying of the freighter, and had inspected each other's cabins, we stood at the rail watching the withdrawal of the gangplank, the casting off, the gap silently appearing, growing definite, widening, between the vessel under our feet and the pilings and the wharf, the dingy brick buildings, the apparently vacant, detached back streets of Brooklyn, and then we shuddered to the bass blasts on the whistle and felt the first vibrations of movement as the vessel was dragged, coming awake, into the channel. We watched the city, suddenly hushed, slipping past us and dropping behind, leaving us, and we were borne along into the widening estuary and looked back to see the gray cliffs receding between the two dark rivers, in the pink glow of the summer evening. The whistle notes from the harbor, the sounds of the horns and sirens from the streets, must have accompanied us part of the way, but they had scarcely seemed audible above the low throb of the freighter's engines and the long trailing syllable of the wake. The whole outbound passage seemed to be enveloped in silence.

We managed to make certain that it was the Liberian flag by looking it up next morning in a book from a glassed bookcase in what the steward referred to grandly as the passengers' lounge, an undefined area at the end of the one long dining table, with a few armchairs and a kind of card table under a thick mat advertising vermouth. The lounge retained all day the odor of an alley running in back of restaurants. The steward was glad to explain that the owners, whoever they really were, had registered the vessel in Liberia for financial and, as he put it, regulatory reasons, to avoid certain taxes and restrictions. That was why, he said, you saw so many ships with Liberian or Panamanian registry, as of course we had. He dropped these nuggets of insider information quickly, out of the side of his mouth, so that they could hardly be heard, to make them sound at once essential and disreputable. It was an effect that clearly had been perfected with practice.

The passengers would come to realize before long that he had a repertoire of small routines, all of them well rehearsed. He ran through several of them in the course of the first day. One that he repeated at every meal, as a ritual of his own, consisted of coming up behind someone at table, with the handle of a tall, tapering, chromium-plated pot in each hand, and asking brightly and loudly, "Café Voir"? Then without waiting for an answer, except perhaps a startled look, he would begin pouring, from a disturbing height, coffee from one spout, cream or milk from the other, managing to hit the cup with both streams remarkably often, though there were occasional wobbles and overshots into saucers and onto the tablecloth. He ignored those in grand style, moving on with the same orotund inquiry to the next speechless diner, without appearing to grasp the nature of his audience's admiration.

* * *

We few passengers had the whole freighter to ourselves, and the boys and I explored it together, a huge, exciting new possession. As the horizon rose and fell I kept telling myself that I was on the way to Europe, and trying to make it credible.

Besides the four of us there was a young couple named Biddle who were on their honeymoon and kept to themselves much of the time, and an older man, a merchant seaman, born in Italy of Italian parents, brought up in the United States. He was on his way to see relatives in Italy, perhaps to ship out on another vessel there, he said, though for the time being he was retired. Questions about the vessel he might be joining or about his relatives led into clouds, but on the other hand he had a way of suddenly starting to tell some episode from his years at sea. His accounts may have been as rehearsed in their way as the steward's skits, and though he told them all as pages of his own life, I came to wonder, as I listened to him, whether some of his anecdotes might not have been tales that he had heard, from somebody else's story, and whether some of them had ever taken place at all. They seldom seemed to connect, at the beginning or end, with something that had happened before and had caused them, or with something that had followed as a consequence. Often they rose out of the silences of our wandering talk, suggested by no association that I could guess. But he told them with confidential immediacy and detail as though they were memories, and I listened to them—and so did Peter if he was around—with rapt attention.

We were headed for Genoa, and he told me that he had sailed out of that port once, in his youth, on a four-masted iron schooner loaded with a full cargo of Carrara marble that was to be delivered far up the Amazon at the suddenly rich city of Manaus, for the palatial new opera house they were building there. It was not their first cargo of that kind, and they had been all the way up the river to Manaus, with marble in the hold, before. But it was in the days before radios were required equipment at sea, or at any rate they had no radio, and it was around the autumn equinox, when weather could turn ugly. It blew hard as they crossed the Mediterranean, and worse after they sailed through the Strait of Gibraltar and started out into the Atlantic. They plowed on under shortened sail, but the storm was violent, and at night the wind and the bucking of the vessel snapped the top of one mast and then another, and the heavy gaffs, whipping at the ends of the stays, swung down, tangled in the rigging, and began to flip and hammer on the side of the schooner and to smash holes in the iron sheeting. The sea started to come in too fast for the pumps to deal with it. They could not signal for help or hope for any, in such seas. The crew took to a lifeboat and pushed off, leaving the schooner to sink with its marble. They managed to reach the African coast in the lifeboat.

Only a few days before, I had listened to another older man, a journalist just back from Brazil, describing Manaus, and the opera house as he had seen it then, with patterns of gray mold clouding its porticos and halls, rotting velvet dangling from walls and balconies, vines twining through the ceilings and over the rows of seats, the jungle reclaiming all that grandiose brief-lived architecture, and I tried to guess how old the seaman might be, and the age of his story. The opera house (I checked later) had been built in the years of the Amazon rubber boom, back in the nineteenth century. Maybe the Italian had heard about it from his grandfather.

Peter was rereading Sherlock Holmes and the Prose Edda, and I think he accorded the seaman's stories a little of the same acceptance. The boys and I played hide-and-seek around the hatches and along the decks, and Peter and I became addicted to lying far out on the bow of the *Nyhorn,* hypnotized by the wave curling up under us, the knife of the prow lifting and sinking, parting the green water.

2

Five summers before that, a little earlier in the year, I was within a week of graduating from a boarding school in Kingston, Pennsylvania, across the river from Wilkes-Barre. Its name was Wyoming Seminary, founded in the 1840s to provide education for the children of Protestant ministers, to whom scholarships were still offered. The original red brick buildings, late neocolonial, with a succession of three white-columned porches and a white belfry, still stood at the corner of tree-lined back streets, with a church (Methodist) across one street and another (Presbyterian) on the street behind the campus. Since my father was a minister, the tuition, I was given to understand, was halved, and I had a working scholarship besides, which paid for my room and board in return for my waiting on table in the dining hall during my first year, and keeping the chemistry laboratory and physics classroom swept out during my second year.

I liked both jobs. The waiters constituted a kind of club, a minor guild, secret society, clan, with mores and a hierarchy, informal but fully understood, and perquisites that included the run of the kitchen. We ate together, serving ourselves, and exchanged knowing gossip in what seemed like a time apart from the tight schedule of the school day. We got out of daily chapel early. We got extra food, including dessert, if we wanted it. But the chemistry job was preferable. It was reserved for seniors, partly, I suppose, because whoever did it must be responsible for working alone. The cleaning was done in the evening, when the study hall on the ground floor had closed, and the big, square, dark red brick building that I associated, for no reason that I can remember, with the end of the Civil War and the presidency of Ulysses Grant, was empty. I had the place to myself. The black counters in the chemistry lab had to be wiped off with a damp cloth, and all the dry, splintery floors of that room, and of the hallway across the top of the stairs, and of the shallow tiers of the lecture room banked upward like a theater, and of the physics room beyond that, had to be sprinkled with an oily granular sawdust dyed green, to lay the dust, and then swept with a wide push broom that I can still hear knocking against the iron legs of the desks with their folded tabletops. The last part, strewing the handfuls of green crumbs ahead of me in arcs, out of a big can, like a sower going forth to sow, went with a somewhat hypnotic slowness, but there was a smooth pleasure in sweeping the floors. When I had finished I could turn out the lights, and by the rays of the distant street lamps filtered in through the trees go to the top level of the sloped room, behind the last row of seats, to lie on the floor looking across at the windows of the girls' dormitory, and with luck catch sight of the girls getting undressed for bed.

That was common or garden voyeurism, but in fact I was in love, and had been since I was nine or ten, with a doctor's daughter in my father's congregation in the Washburn Street Presbyterian Church in Scranton, with whom I was so shy that I could scarcely speak to her when I had a chance to get near her. During the last year when I was at Seminary, she had been sent to stay with friends of her family in a house just across the street behind the school, on the other side of the grass hockey lawn, where I could just see her house through the trees from my dormitory window. But it was forbidden to leave the campus except for short, prescribed periods. Our outings were watched. There was no way to reach her by telephone or to set up meetings, because she too was severely restricted. I saw her only a few times when we managed it half by chance. It seemed that we had known each other for a very long time, and that unrecorded history was like a secret understanding between us, and it gave me hope. I had not been allowed to invite girls out on dates or take them to movies when I was in grade school or high school. I had seen her then only in choir practice at the church, and on Sunday evenings after Christian Endeavor, when sometimes we gathered at each other's houses (and occasionally, if my father was not likely to find out about it, we danced). Once I had been allowed to invite her to take a hike with me on a Saturday afternoon, and we had set out, my heart pounding, but partway up the mountain I realized that my fly was completely open. It was unbuttoned—that was in the days before zippers—and that crucially altered the tone of the outing, because I was too mortified to find a way to get my fly buttoned without calling attention to it, and when I spoke to her I stood sideways or talked over my shoulder.

I was not sure at first why she had been sent to stay with that family in the big house across the street behind the school. She was reluctant to talk about it and seemed unhappy but determined not to admit it. In the end she gave me to understand that her father wanted her to be there so that she would be able to go out with a young man a few years older than we were, who lived in Wilkes-Barre and came from a family with a considerable amount of money and social position in the region. I had always thought of her father as wealthy. They were the richest family in the church and he was an eminent figure in the city, but evidently his ambition was far from satisfied. I knew from what she told me then that despite her apparent self-assurance she was afraid of her father, and I understood that well enough, because for years, until I turned on him physically and defied him, I had been afraid of mine. During my early childhood he had been distant, unpredictable, and harsh. He had punished me fiercely for things I had not known were forbidden, when the list of known restrictions was already long and oppressive. I was told regularly that I loved him, as I was told that I loved God and Jesus, and I did not know at the time that the names for much of my feeling about him were really dread and anger.

But by the time I went to Seminary, at fourteen, he was in Europe as a chaplain in the army. In his absence I had transformed him in my mind into the figure I wanted to believe he was, and without my realizing that it was happening, I had transferred much of my resentment of him to the school and its antique restrictions. When he came back to the States after the war, I spent a week or so with him at the army base at Fort Story, Virginia, a time of reacquaintance and acceptance that would eventually help me to ponder elements of his past that may have fostered some of the hapless, incapacitating anxieties he carried with him.

At Seminary, the faculty kept a stern, suspicious eye on the budding adolescents of both sexes living under its one roof. Boys were not allowed to speak to girls on campus, except for one period of half an hour or so, once or twice a week, when they could "socialize" in one designated "socializing room," in the presence of the white-haired Dean of Women. The elder members of the faculty mounted guard over the priceless distance between the sexes of the boarding students. I did not get home very often on weekends, and had no money when I did escape from the campus, and I found the regimentation suffocating. By the end of spring, that last year, I had been admitted to Princeton with a scholarship, and during the final weeks, as the sentiment about leaving the dear old

walls intensified among some of my classmates, I could not wait
to see the last of the place.

In the final weeks there, though, the weather was beautiful.
The big trees were reentering the sounds and smells of true summer. One weekend when the year's studies were all but over and
the classrooms empty, and I had been confined to campus as a dis-
ciplinary measure for some rebellious infraction, I was earning
points or payment by washing the outsides of the windows on the
upper floors of the main class building, with one other boy. We
had straps with swivel hooks to hold us in place as we stood on the
cement window sills, up among the rustling leaves, watching the
street and the campus from the birds' height. The sense of risk,
the recurrent rush of vertigo, nourished an elation, a foretaste
of freedom, a floating happiness that accompanied me, and my
bucket, reflected in the panes of window after window, and stayed
with me as we carried the buckets and squeegees and rags down
the marble stairs and as I went across the street to the dormitories
and upstairs to my room. It was a feeling that remained beside me
as though I could touch it, through those last days, and it was
there one sunny morning when a large, heavy boy, a guard on the
football team and neighbor in the dormitory, came crashing up the
stairs. I heard the roar of his voice well before I could make out
what he was shouting about. I ran out to hear what was so important as he pounded along the hall, and others popped out of their
doorways around him. "They've landed," he kept shouting,
"they've landed." It was the Normandy landing. It had just begun.
Few boys had radios, but some had been hiding them until then,
and all at once they were turned on everywhere, and the remnants
of the school schedule were forgotten as we huddled around
them.

3

That winter I had read *War and Peace,* carrying the thick red volume down the hall to the bathroom after lights out and sitting there in a marble stall for hours, unless I was caught, by some professor on his rounds, completely immersed in the Russia of the Romantic era, the Napoleonic invasion, the characters and dilemmas of Tolstoy's huge fiction, and also in Tolstoy's essays, set at intervals in the narrative, on the nature of history, the forces that impel it. I had never encountered that kind of speculation. I found it enthralling, and had been discussing Tolstoy's theories with my history teacher, Prof. Leroy Bugbee, one of the two professors there whom I really liked. The other was my Spanish teacher, Prof. Lawrence Sampson, who was dying of a weak heart and puffed cheerfully along the street with a cane, stopping to catch his breath, but whose wit, temperament, cultivation, and skeptical worldliness awakened in me a growing fascination with languages and language. He taught me my first years of Spanish. I had been reading some of Frost's poems, and Shakespeare, and had won the Declamation Contest (twenty-five dollars) with a performance of Mark Anthony's speech over Caesar's body in *Julius Caesar*. But it was Tolstoy's story that went on playing in my head into the months of that spring and summer when I had turned sixteen, and bits of news were reaching us from the war in Europe.

While my father was overseas in the army, my mother had taken an administrative job in the Scranton YWCA. We had moved from the manse, across the street from my father's church on Washburn Street, to an apartment on the other side of town, on Madison. Most university schedules had been speeded up as a wartime measure, with three semesters a year and no summer vacations, and so, a few weeks after I graduated from Seminary, a friend of my mother's named Deb Borden, who taught Physical Education at the "Y" and had a little ten-year-old Ford, drove my mother and me and my things down to Princeton. I had a suitcase or two and a few books, but the car did not have much room in it, and Deb could not see why I needed so much *stuff*.

At the registration office in Stanhope Hall I was directed to Dodd Hall, a late nineteenth-century stone building with fire escapes that amounted to balconies, and splintery floors, broad staircases, and iron banisters inside. The assigned rooms, up one flight, consisted of an entrance hall, and inside that a large living room with a fireplace, and two bedrooms, one on either side of the entrance. I would be sharing the quarters with another boy who had just graduated from Seminary, where I had never known him. He had been a day student. He was very blond, pale, Teutonic, and turned out to be intensely earnest and conventional. He was already determined to become a doctor, like his successful father. He had not yet arrived when I got there.

There was no furniture. We had been informed at the registration office that we could pick up secondhand pieces at several places across Nassau Street, and though my mother was naturally suspicious of buying anything of that kind because you never knew where it had been, on the basis of that official advice she and Deb and I walked to one of the jumbled exchanges, and my mother bought a few matured essentials—bed, desk, chairs, tables, lamps—while visibly struggling to overcome her distaste at their condition, especially when it came to the mattress, which necessitated a patient reassurance, from the person running the establishment, about what every mattress there had endured to restore its innocence, and about how this was the way it was always done. According to the law, he said, which seemed to reassure her somewhat. Deb stood apart from the whole undertaking, somewhere above it. It seemed to me that it was my mother who was being initiated, misgiving by misgiving, into the unkempt rites that were the prerequisites of becoming a college student, and that to me somehow they must already be familiar.

The furniture we had settled on was to be delivered in the next few hours. My mother kept clucking her tongue and remembering that she had always heard that Princeton was awfully *fast*. She announced that the rooms were utterly filthy, and the next stop, after the veteran furniture had been settled on, was a hardware store, where she bought a bucket, a scrub brush, cloths, ammonia, white vinegar, and washing soda, and on the way back to the room she made sure I understood the correct mixture of them that was to be used, in *hot* water, to get the buff-colored paintwork clean. We must have had a sandwich somewhere—one that she had made at home and packed in waxed paper—before they left to drive back to Scranton, which seemed a very long way in those days. As I began to scrub, alone in the rooms, I thought I felt the arrival of the beginning of freedom. The Promised Land was empty and evidently dirty, but I was elated, and when my roommate, whose name was Alex, arrived, the furniture was piled in the middle of the room and I was obediently sloshing the wainscots for the first and only time, before I knocked off to push the battered pieces into place for a new life, in which Alex would be shocked, day by day, by my views about everything.

He was a couple of years older than I was, but then, at sixteen, I was young to be there at all. Back in grade school, in Union City, New Jersey, I had been moved a grade ahead, skipping a year, and then another one, and then had been told that that would not work because I was too much younger than any of my classmates, which would be bad for me, and I had been moved back again one grade. I came to feel that somehow all that shifting was my fault. After it was settled there was always an age difference of a year or two between my classmates and me.

4

After I left Seminary I had learned that, in the weeks that followed the Normandy landings, the Germans, thrown onto the defensive, drew units from occupied territories, particularly from southern France and northern Italy, to build up strength for a battle that they hoped would throw the Allies back into the sea. I heard odds and ends about it over the radio, read scraps of stories in the occasional newspapers, and we talked about it around the school during the days before graduation, and on the picnics with friends who had cars and could drive out to nearby lakes. We did not have much real information, and the news was kept off-stage much of the time by the impending graduation itself, the visiting families, our own sense of imminent change, and our moving out of the old dormitory building—its long swaybacked halls with their brown linoleum floors and naked overhead bulbs, shadowy at all hours with the ghosts of generations going back to the Civil War and before it. Then we would hear of the war again: fragmentary accounts of the fighting in Normandy, silent and unreal. Impersonal dispatches about the advances, the continuing bombardments, the German buildup. I am sure it did not occur to me that I would go on hearing details of those days, those far-off events, for years, and in fact for the rest of my life.

The Germans hoped to rout the advancing Allies near the city of Caen, east of Bayeux and the landing beaches, and as they fell back they were preparing defensive positions and assembling troops, artillery, and armor for the battle. The Luftwaffe had been crippled by then, so they could no longer count on air support as they had done in the early days of the war, at the time of the British evacuation of the beaches at Dunkerque. The Germans based their hopes, in great part, on the numbers and performance of their tanks, and crack German units—armored units especially —were being rushed north and west for the decisive confrontation. The troop movements toward Caen were part of a general ebbing of German forces out of southern Europe to concentrate on defending the north. As the Germans retreated through southern France, with certain picked units such as the Das Reich Division perpetrating vindictive farewell massacres on the way, the French Resistance, which had long been organizing for this moment, did whatever it could to ambush and harass and delay them, at times with telling success, but often at terrible cost to themselves, and to nearby civilian populations, whom the Nazis punished in retribution for the activities and the very survival of the Resistance.

A small number of British and American agents had been hidden in the French countryside for a year and more, helping to maintain contact between the Allied command and the French Resistance network, and in the days after the Normandy landings others were parachuted into the south, to provide liaison and to help, where that might be possible. One of these agents, as I understood the story (though it was told in so sidelong and elusive a manner that I was never sure exactly what did happen), was Alan Stuyvesant, a direct descendant of Peter Stuyvesant, "Peg-Leg

Pete," the Dutch seventeenth-century governor of New Amsterdam, which after the English took it would be called New York.

When I came to know Alan I had just turned twenty and he was forty-seven. Although I had graduated from Princeton and was in graduate school and married, I was still provincial, naïve, and penniless. And Alan, a generation older, was worldly, knowledgeable, opinionated, and very rich. He had learned, long before that, how to appear to be frank and open, while referring to his own life with a practiced reserve, recounting moments of it with a flourish of humor, as finished anecdotes, and then stepping aside from them into the wings. It was a while before I learned to recognize the maneuver, and to see that his descriptions of his brother's and his mother's drunken binges and turns of unedifying behavior were cutouts: mythologized fragments held up in front of him in a way that was meant to suggest his own amiable candor about matters that he knew someone would reveal sooner or later, in any case. My own upbringing had not fostered an aptitude for asking pertinent questions. I had been told repeatedly that it was rude to be openly curious about anything "personal." Besides that, I am still surprised to learn how many things other people who have known each other for years, and perhaps at close quarters, have never found out about each other.

It is not hard to understand why Alan might have been chosen for a liaison mission with the French Resistance in Provence near the Italian border. He was bilingual, to begin with. His mother had been the Belgian Princesse de Caraman-Chimay. (I never managed to find out much about his father, who for some reason or other was not talked about.) Alan had grown up partly in France and had gone to French schools. From his mother he had inherited a large villa on the sea cliff at St. Jean Cap-Ferrat, between Nice and Monte Carlo, which had been her summer house for many years. It was a house where he had spent summers during his childhood. He had known the Alpes Maritimes all his life.

The story, as I understood it, was that in the summer of 1944

Alan had been dropped by parachute into a small valley north of Nice to join a man whom he already knew well, from very different, urbane circumstances. That man's code name in the Resistance was Captain Goderville. The name by which Alan knew him was Jean Prévost. Prévost was a man of letters, a writer and literary critic of some eminence. In 1944 he was forty-three years old, roughly the same age as Alan. He had been born in St. Pierre-les-Nemours, south of Fontainebleau, and at the age of seventeen had entered the Lycée Henri IV as a student, in a special category chosen to study for a competitive examination. His philosophy professor was the well-known writer and essayist who published under the name of "Alain." Jean began to write, and was publishing articles in *La Nouvelle Revue Française* by the time he was twenty-three. He married two years later. His wife, Marcelle Auclair, was also a writer. They had three children, Michel, Françoise, and Alain, named for Jean's professor, who had remained a family friend. In the early thirties Jean lectured at Cambridge and travelled to the United States. His first marriage came apart and he remarried when he was thirty-nine. In 1943, after the fall of France, he obtained his Doctorate of Letters and was awarded the Grand Prix of the Académie Française for a study of Stendhal.

In that same year, 1943, he joined the Resistance, undertook several missions in Paris, and in 1944 took command of a company of the *Maquis* in the Vercors, a mountainous region that became a famous operational area of the Resistance. On June 13th of that year, one week after the first Normandy landings, on a winding mountain road near St. Nizier du Moucherotte, his company ambushed and repulsed the German 157th *Gebirgsjager* Division. Fighting continued there in the mountains until the Maquis withdrew on July 23rd. Jean had been wounded. He and some of his company hid in a cave, the Grotte des Fées, where the Germans found them on August 1st, and Jean was killed.

At what point in 1944 Alan Stuyvesant made contact with him, if that is what really happened, I have never been completely sure. Alan had known Jean, and Jean's first wife, and their children, in Paris, and his friendship with Marcelle and the children continued after the war. Alan said that Jean had asked him to promise to look after the children if he did not survive the war. It is hard to imagine such a promise being requested and given before the war. The most likely time for that would have been at a meeting between them when Jean was in the Resistance, just before the action in early June 1944. But Alan's vagueness about the circumstances made me curious—to no avail—about how it had come about. Only once, when several of us were driving to dinner from St. Jean Cap-Ferrat to St. Paul de Vence, at an intersection north of Nice Alan pointed to a road we were not taking and said that it was "up that way" that he had been dropped in by parachute, and Jean had been wounded, and caught by the Germans, and killed. It sounded as though the place was just a few miles up the road, and it was years before I pieced the dates and names of sites together and realized that the region he had been talking about was most of the way to Grenoble, a distance of many miles through the mountains.

It was because of Alan's promise, and Jean's youngest son, Alain, that I would go to Europe.

5

With the stepped-up schedule that had continued at the university through the end of the war and for a while afterward, I had graduated in 1947, three years after I entered as an undergraduate. Then I had gone on to graduate school in Romance languages and embarked upon my thoughtless first marriage.

In early youth everything is untried, and one thing may not seem any more surprising than the rest. I know that when I first found myself at Princeton I did not at once appreciate how incongruous it was for me to be there, of all places. To begin with there was the matter of money. I had none. At Wyoming Seminary I had had an allowance of a dollar a month, which did not matter so much there since there was nowhere to spend it except one ice cream parlor near the school, and ice cream cones in those days cost five or ten cents. At Princeton, in recognition of my new status, my allowance was stepped up to a dollar a week. My mother apparently had conferred by letter with my father about it, and they had arrived at that figure and believed it was adequate, and I said nothing about it. I had grown up knowing that they got by on very little, and it would have gone against the grain for me to ask for money.

Although my father was a Presbyterian minister, he had not finished at any of the schools he attended, from the one-room country schoolhouse in Rimerton, Pennsylvania, to Western Seminary in Pittsburgh. He had begun his ministry at small, rural churches in western Pennsylvania, and when he was thirty-one, a year or so before I was born, he had accepted a "call" to a big church in Union City, New Jersey, on top of the Palisades overlooking Hoboken and the river, with the Manhattan skyline as its backdrop. We lived there until the year I was nine. Union City must have seemed a great step up in the world when he and my mother went there. The First Presbyterian Church (there was only one) was a tall, yellow-brick, turn-of-the-century structure, with two steeples, a rose window, and green carpets down the sloping aisles. But its heyday, whatever that may have amounted to, was already irretrievably behind it. "Foreigners," as we kept hearing, and Catholics, were taking over the whole area. The congregation that had built the church and attended it was ebbing away, almost gone, and the church's financial stability with it. By the time my father became the pastor there, everything about the church from the attendance to the condition of the building was in steep decline. He invested in a new glass-fronted poster display-case out in front of the building to announce the services and sermon titles. Then the Great Depression hit. I remember being wheeled through the streets, in the big brown wicker baby carriage, at a different pace than usual, picking up a feeling of urgency and anxiety when I breathed, and stopping to look up, along with a small crowd of people, at the closed, polished bronze bank doors, and hearing crying and voices full of grief and anguish above me, a scene that I did not understand but that would resurface at times as an emblem. We stayed on in Union City for several years after that, through the first years of my childhood. Not long after we left there, the church building was sold—to the *Catholics*—and a few years after that it was torn down.

The move to Scranton, then, and the Washburn Street Presbyterian Church, was something of a repetition of the earlier step to Union City. Again it must have seemed like a marked improvement in worldly success. The church was a large, imposing building with a square, crenellated belfry tower, and across the street from it was the twelve-room frame manse. My mother was immediately struck by the fact that the manse had thirty-six large windows—she counted them—which would need curtains. A committee of welcomers, made up of church elders and members of the board of trustees, spoke of the church and the city in glowing terms, and delegates talked over plans for redecorating the manse. It was summertime. The streetcars celloed and swung along the tree-lined streets near Elm Park, and the new "call" to Scranton at first seemed to represent a new life.

But Scranton was deep in its own depression, within the national one. The anthracite mines had all but lost their long struggle with the cheaper soft coal from shallower mines near Pittsburgh and in West Virginia. Silk manufacturing, and then the artificial silk industry, which had been the hope of the Chamber of Commerce in the twenties, had collapsed. The church finances reflected those of the region, and before long my father and senior members of the board of trustees were locked in opposition, mostly about money, as far as I could tell. His stipulated salary had been miserably small to begin with—three hundred dollars a month, three thousand six hundred a year—and the trustees' rancor built until they stopped paying it altogether, a move that led to the matter being carried to the Synod of the Presbyterian Church, which forced the trustees to pay what they owed or have the church closed down. But the deep dissension, the subsequent rift in the congregation, remained there and affected my father's moods and behavior at home. For months at a time my mother managed the household on almost no money, and the persistent lack of it, along with the unquestioned necessity (as we were taught) of keeping up appearances as "the preacher's family," became a condition of life in those years.

6

My father was severe in any case, and capriciously so, and the uncertainties and anxiety of his situation at Scranton, his fear of failure, of being found out as someone with no real education or credentials, must have depressed him and damaged an already disappointed marriage. He kept talking about insurance, and when he got paid anything he put as much as he could into endowment policies, speaking of what he was doing as a sacrificial burden but an act of foresight. His attention to me was limited almost entirely to what I was forbidden to do. The list seemed unique (if compared with what my schoolmates were allowed to do), and it was absolute. Punishments for infractions were sudden, without appeal, and relatively harsh. He spent almost no time with me, and when he did we had little to say to each other.

Some of my discontent and claustrophobia in those years took the form of feeling far away from water. I remembered the glimpse of the Hudson River that we had had from the bottom of 4th Street in Union City, looking across Palisade Avenue past my father's church, and the time or two when my father had allowed

me to accompany him to his small, crammed, musty, dusty study
at the top of the steep, narrow, boxed-in spiral stairs out of the
vestry in the back of the church. One window of the study looked
out over Hoboken and the harbor and the river, with the ferries
coming and going, the freighters and liners catching the west
light, and beyond them the jagged, gray, glittering skyline of New
York, looming in its silent distance, its own dimension. I had been
allowed to accompany him on those occasions "if I thought I
could keep quiet while he worked on his sermon. Did I think I
could?" I thought I could, and I knelt on the blue velvet cushion on
the window seat, gazing out through the leaded panes, or through
the open casements—though usually his windows were tightly
closed—watching the river, without a word, utterly rapt in the
vast scene out in front of me, hearing my father muttering words
of scripture ("Thou fool, this night shall thy *soul* be required of
thee") somewhere far behind me. Whole trains were crossing the
river on railroad ferries, all shades of orange in the sunlight. White
puffs of steam climbed out of unseen whistles and horns, the distant sounds arriving, faint and faded, a long breath afterward. I
was seeing something that I could not reach and that would never
go away.

The French liner *Normandie,* said to be a vessel of incomparable
beauty, was berthed in Hoboken, and my father took me there
once to see it, stopping at the house of someone affiliated with
the neighboring Baptist church, whose pastor was a friend of my
father's. The man was a barber, merry and red-faced, his barber-
shop in a brownstone building facing the harbor, and there was a
parrot next door belonging to a friend of his. The barber took us
to the *Normandie* and we stared up at the tapered, towering prow
looming high over us, but no one was allowed aboard that day,
and the mysterious disaster that led to the ship's capsizing at the
dock happened not long afterward.

The German behemoth *Leviathan* (my father pronounced it

with a dramatic emphasis on the "i") was still there too. That ship had been impounded, my father said, during the World War. He wanted to see it partly because of the passage about the Leviathan in the Book of Job, and partly, I think, because of his own experiences in his youth as a sailor on a mine sweeper during the war. It was possible then to get permission to see something of the *Leviathan,* and we went down one day to the vast, dark, empty, echoing wharf building, where we were met by a man who seemed all but wordless. He led us across a gangplank over the black water, and then along dim iron corridors, up stairs to a dingy deck, the screams of gulls, the smell of the harbor, and back again. My father began to talk about Jonah.

Four destroyers were berthed for a while where we could see them from the Palisades, and the public was invited aboard to tour them. My father took me along to see them one afternoon, and we lined up with a small group and were led by men in real naval uniforms, between rope railings, from the wharf to the gangplank, and then across the decks of all four ships, and were shown the torpedo tubes, and then led back again. My father talked affectionately about his mine sweeper, and one voyage as far as Cuba and the Panama Canal, and how they had always thrown all the uneaten food and other supplies overboard before coming into port, so that they could order more, and the waste of war. Oh my.

Hanging in the church basement were two very large framed photographs of battleships, old ones, with towers like round black baskets, dotted with blurry white shapes of sailors. The brass plates under the names (USS *Texas?* and the older *Arizona?*) said they had twelve Babcock and Wilcox boilers, I believe. My father said he was not sure why they were there. Somebody must have given them to the church. They seemed no stranger than my father sailing on a mine sweeper. The harbor, and the river, made it all credible.

The first summer that we were in Scranton, a member of the

congregation arranged for us to rent for very little money (as I overheard) a ramshackle, homemade cottage in the woods an hour's drive north of the city, beyond Elk Mountain, at Fiddle Lake. For a month or so the days there seemed like a complete time, with an age of its own. The friend who had found it for us drove my sister and me up there in the back of his plumber's truck, and that in itself was a great adventure for us. We arrived among the tall trees to the cawing of crows, which made my heart pound with excitement, and tears, to my surprise and embarrassment, come to my eyes. During the week my father was back in Scranton much of the time—leaving his list of prohibitions hanging in the air—and my sister and I were there with our mother, who loyally observed the injunctions, more or less ("Now you know your father said not to do that"), where they concerned our safety. I loved the lake, the rowboat, the sunlit rippled sand in the shallows, the cold clay springs out deeper, the old trees along the shore, and all that they allowed me to imagine, as I had never loved anywhere up until then, and I counted the days there, trying to keep them from slipping away.

The next summer at Fiddle Lake, one day I spotted a rowboat sunk on the lake bottom, and I waded back to it later with a friend, to investigate. It was filled with rocks, only a foot or two below the surface, an elephant in its graveyard. I got the rocks out, and with the help of a boy next door dragged the water-logged hulk ashore and overturned it to dry out a bit. The craft had never been a model of grace in its best days. The stern had been sawn off and crudely replaced. Just the same it was my new treasure, a vessel to dream about. It would be a sailboat. Nobody at the lake had a sailboat then. It would be a sloop, with one, or even two jibs, and a bowsprit, and a deck up forward.

That winter I thought of it all the time, getting books about boats out of the public library. There had to be a keel. I talked a house builder from the church into bolting a sheet of iron into a slot in a long block of wood that could, in turn, be bolted to the bottom of the boat. I pored over the Sears Roebuck catalogue for essential materials for which I saved up my ten-cents-a-week allowance. Canvas for sails was a dollar a square yard, and then there was heavy thread, a sailor's palm for stitching, caulking for the joints, white deck paint. I cut the cloth, when it came in the mail, and stitched the sails, with the sections laid out on the living room floor. Mr. Yoder, a retired school superintendent in the church who loved to make things at his forge and anvil, made me a set of iron rings for the mainsail.

Two houses down the street, at the corner of Washburn and South Main Avenue, old Mrs. Davis with her floor-length black dresses and her white hair piled on her head, who had lived on alone in her big, elaborate, dark house—"the mansion," as it was called in the neighborhood, with turrets and round rooms, and balconies and porches and banisters wound around it upstairs and down—had died, and the house had been sold to be torn down and replaced by an Esso station. I watched the progress day by day: the funeral, the emptiness afterward, the emptying of the emptiness, the demolition and the razing, the opening of the cellars, the excavation with a steam shovel for the gasoline tanks, and then the rise of the cement building, faced finally with enameled white metal panels. I stood watching the work, after school and on Saturdays, and got to be on nodding terms with some of the workmen, and when they began to use tar on some of the surfaces they were paving I managed to buy or cadge a big square cookie tin full of tar, with a wire to carry it by, to use for the bottom of the boat after I had caulked the joints in accordance with the instructions in the Sea Scout Manual.

Mr. Yoder had been intrigued by the thought of the derelict rowboat that I was transforming—in my mind—into a sailboat, and without saying anything about it he had made me a perfect anchor, complete to the tapering heart-shaped flukes. It weighed almost forty pounds. He gave it to me sometime that next spring —partly to please my father, I think, for Mr. Yoder had been one of his loyal supporters on the board of trustees—and it became at once one of my most prized possessions, an epitome of the whole enterprise. I can still hear the sound of the iron ring striking against the shaft.

When we went up to the lake that summer I caulked and tarred the bottom of the boat, found someone to help me get the keel bolted on, got the decking nailed across it with a socket for the mast, and then painted everything white—three coats. Finally one day, with the help of the boy next door, I managed to get the boat into the water again, found out where it still leaked (clear water appearing as though by magic through the tar and new paint), and patched it some more. I put on the rudder, stepped the mast, and hoisted the mainsail with the halyard running through clothesline pulleys that I had bought in the hardware store at the corner. I had named this ponderous aspiring swan *Zephyr*, and had embroidered a winged figure, a hybrid part dolphin and part torpedo, on the sail, imitating my mother's cross-stitch, but with no practice or gift for it. The anchor took up most of the space before the mast and made it hard to hoist the jib. Or jibs. I pushed away from the dock and sat in the cockpit, holding the sheet and the tiller. There was no wind, to start with. When a little came across the lake the boat had even less sense about sailing than I did. *Zephyr's* preferred motion turned out to be sideways. The sails helped us drift with the wind, leaving small dimples across the smooth surface we were sliding away from, along an expanse as wide as the boat's length, which was eleven feet. Fortunately I had kept the old oarlocks and had borrowed a pair of oars, which got us back after a while, to start making adjustments. The vision of the craft's eventual skimming flight was unimpaired, for the time being.

For my thirteenth birthday my mother gave me *A Conrad Argosy*, a compendium of Joseph Conrad's stories and short novels, which expanded and colored all my fantasies of sails and sailing. I decided that I would sail *Zephyr* down the Delaware River, all the way, and then up the Jersey shore and on up the East River, to Cape Cod. At the same time the book kindled ambitions of another kind. The first page of *Heart of Darkness* seized me in a spell, and as I read I longed to be able to write, and I began to try.

That was the winter the Japanese attacked Pearl Harbor. I had the radio turned on in my bedroom, very low so as not to disturb my father, and I heard the news. Everyone was already talking of the armed services, of uniforms, and I was, as usual, too young. In the attic I had a pile of *National Geographics*, and in one of them there was an article on Annapolis, with pictures of cadets in summer dress uniforms, and I thought of the doctor's daughter and how she would look upon me if I were wearing summer whites, and for the next couple of years I wanted to go to Annapolis, and everyone around me, I suppose, humored the idea, which no doubt they thought so improbable as to be harmless. In retrospect, that ambition seems to me to have been, above all, an image of an underlying determination to get away.

7

After America entered the war my father enlisted in the army as a chaplain. During the summer before he left he rowed *Zephyr* across the lake to the cottage of friends from the congregation, for them to plant purple petunias in. I was awarded a scholarship to Wyoming Seminary and went off to boarding school, coming home sometimes for the weekend on the small two-car Luzerne Valley Line. My sister followed a year later, and my mother moved from the manse, across town, to be near her job at the Y, but it was she who continued to hold us together. In my last year at Seminary I took the College Entrance Examination, rather as a matter of course, without any clear idea of what it might lead to. I was fifteen. I was still hoping, more or less by habit, to go to the Naval Academy, dreaming of the doctor's daughter, but I was too young in any case, and in the meantime I was advised by one of my professors that it would be a good thing to take the examination.

It was held in a public room upstairs over a dry-goods store (where as students we had stolen pairs of socks on a dare) at a corner of the main street a block from the school. Through the open windows I could smell the new leaves of spring. There were only a few students taking the examination that year, most of them girls, as I recall. On the top of the examination form there was a line where the applicant was to write the names of the colleges for which he or she was taking the test and applying for entrance. I thought of the prospect of a year of college as a way of getting some preliminary schooling that would help me later at Annapolis, but even so, when I had to name colleges or universities, I realized that I knew only the names of football teams and engineering schools. I wrote down Lehigh and MIT (despite the fact that math had always been my weakest subject), thinking of preparing for Annapolis. And I had heard my parents talk about Princeton, so I wrote Princeton. I learned, some time after the examination, that the Princeton my parents had been talking about with memorable respect was not the university at all but the Presbyterian theological seminary. My examination pages, fortunately, went to the university anyway, and when I got the results, my score was acceptable at all the colleges listed. Princeton offered me a scholarship besides, and a history professor at the Seminary said that if I was really thinking of going to the Naval Academy with its emphasis on math and the physical sciences it would be a good idea to devote the intervening year to the humanities while I had a chance to. I went to Princeton.

By the summer of 1944 civilian students on the Princeton campus were a small minority among military trainees in the v-5 and v-12 programs. (These were officer training programs, and I knew what the designations meant at the time, but I have forgotten.) Older men were there in the AMGOT (Allied Military Government of Occupied Territory) program, which was preparing business and professional men to run countries liberated from the Nazis as soon as the war was over. The servicemen sat in on some of the lectures with the civilians, but they marched in formations around the campus and otherwise lived apart. The eating clubs, which had been the setting of Princeton's elitist ("fast," as my mother said) social life in the years between the wars, were closed, except for Tiger Club, which was used as a dining hall for the few civilian students, and Prospect, next door, as a kind of sitting room. At Tiger, as part of my working scholarship, I waited on table. The small number of civilians, and the fact that most of us were in one way or another irregulars, either physically unfit for military service or too young to be called up, obscured for a while how incongruous it was for me, and for others of my friends on scholarships, to be virtually or completely penniless in a university famous for its rich, privileged student body and mores. By the time I had been there for two semesters, so many of the civilian students had been called up, as they turned eighteen, to go into uniform, that only 143 were left in my class.

The old red sandstone library, on the eve of being shunted aside by the construction of the new one nearby, was at once a capacious, spellbinding realm. The stacks were open, the building remained open late, and my reading led me to further curiosity, new names and subjects and lives. I noted them down, perused the card catalogues looking them up, prowled the glass-floored walkways between the stacks, and made my way back to my room laden with books. I read far outside the assignments, and often on wild tangents, forgetting the assignments themselves, from which I had been distracted by siren allusions. It was the literature courses that held and then impelled me, but I must have been exasperating to most of my professors.

Most of my social life, during the first semesters there, consisted of friendships with other scholarship students, many of whom waited on table, first at Tiger Club, and later on, when the civilian student body began to expand again, in the high-ceilinged neo-Gothic dining hall known as the Commons. It was there, one August evening, that I turned up to put on my white waiter's jacket and eat with the other waiters before dinner and found them excitedly discussing something called the atomic bomb, which the United States had dropped on Japan. At first I thought it was a movie they were talking about, or a new work of science fiction, or a sinister joke. When I realized that they were serious and learned details of what they were talking about, I felt a wave of cold, then of disbelief and denial, reactions that have affected the world ever since that evening.

Some of my friends still looked very young, and others had obvious physical handicaps that made it clear why they were not in the service while the war was on, but not all of the reasons for their being out of uniform were apparent. One evening I stood waiting in a movie queue in town, with a tall, robust-looking friend, talking about our shared passion for Thomas Mann. My friend had an incurable kidney disease. (At that age, utterly unable to confront or imagine such a thing, we pretended to ignore it, and so I have felt ever since that I must have seemed unaware of it, or even indifferent to it, and I feel now how inadequate whatever I said to him about it was. He died of the disease a year or so later.) A small, white-haired birdy lady behind us suddenly reached up to tap my friend on the arm, and asked, "Young man, why aren't you in the service?" He smiled down at her indulgently and said, "I have syphilis, madam."

Among the remaining civilians there were a few hard-drinking, high-living types used to having money and spending it, who discoursed at length about their wild weekends in New York or Washington. Some of them sported Confederate flags above their mantelpieces and left their doors standing open. There was a silent gulf between these relics of the school's country-club legend and the shabbier, nerdier, motley skeleton crew on working scholarships. Then there were exceptions who were neither one nor the other, afloat between both, more serious and disenchanted than the tyro playboys, and far more worldly-wise than the likes of us. They were older than we were, rare and singular, returning to university life after something else. There were the first few returning veterans. Some of those were silent. But one was a former navy fighter pilot whose room was across the hall from mine. He told tall stories about smuggling operations using the fighter plane on trips between the Caribbean and the States. He was amiable, skeptical about everything, a legendary and apparently unbeatable poker player, hospitable with his neighbors in the dormitory, generous and open—except that he had a whole other life somewhere in New York, to which he departed on weekends, and of which he said nothing at all. Another became a kind of elder brother figure for a few of us who were already dreaming of being writers. His name was Bunkley. He was the son of an admiral and had been a journalist in Argentina. He had published revelations about the government there that led to his having to skip the country, and he had barely made it. His fragmentary references to that time were redolent of the violence that we were hearing about from the world at large. He was a hard drinker whose liquor cabinet was open to his friends, a brilliant talker, a disillusioned student of history and literature, a young man grown up and desperate. He killed himself a couple of years later, playing Russian roulette at a party, in front of his girlfriend. Those few elders seemed to us fully mature, emblems of worldly wisdom from a generation that was almost our own.

The abnormally small number of civilian students, as we realized even at the time, had given to the campus a feeling of space that it probably had not had for years, and that would soon be completely forgotten. On my allowance an occasional movie was just possible, but even the most frugal trips to New York were out of the question. Once during those years I hitchhiked as far as Newark with another waiter, a boy from Missouri who had never been to New York. We made it to the Newark railroad station and got the train to Grand Central for seventeen cents each, managed to pick up a pair of pretty high-school students, twins, on 42nd

Street, and take them for a cup of coffee. Then we had just enough
for the train tickets back to Newark.

But on one of my early explorations of the wartime campus
I discovered, below the stadium, the riding hall, apparently deserted,
and beyond it a stable with about a dozen horses. They included,
as I learned, polo ponies, quarter horses, and Morgans, all under
the eye of a depressed retired jockey sitting in the tack room by
himself, out of his mind with boredom. The horses spent much of
the day in stall. I asked him whether they did not need exercise,
and he said of course they did. I asked whether I might be allowed
to ride them, and he asked whether I could ride. I mustered up
images of penny pony rides in Nay Aug Park in Scranton, and of
being seated, years before that, high up on top of a white plow
horse and led around the barnyard, and I said yes. He may have
guessed the extent of my experience, but he saddled up Red, the
biggest, oldest, slowest horse in the stable, good-hearted old Red,
giving me pointers as he did it, and led Red and me into the empty
riding hall with its light like the inside of a paper bag, and he
watched me mount, adjusted the stirrups, and left me to it. For a
week or two Red and I spent an hour or two almost every afternoon circling the vacant arena, with Red understanding the situation perfectly and willing to humor me, in an absentminded way.
Then I was allowed to try other horses—polo ponies, a quarter
horse—first inside the halls and eventually outside it, in the corral.
Finally I was allowed to ride out off the campus into the patches
of overgrown meadow and the woods that ran along the shore of
Lake Carnegie almost the whole way to Kingston, at that time. A
quarter horse named Bobby, trained as an officer's mount, was my
favorite. He was nearly black, with his roached mane growing
back, and the shaved patch on his neck with his serial number disappearing under the last of his winter coat. I am sure that Bobby,
like Red and the polo ponies I sometimes rode, grasped at once
all they needed to know about my abilities as a rider, and perhaps

recognized aspects of my character that I had managed not to acknowledge. Bobby tried a few tricks at the beginning, such as veering suddenly toward low-hanging tree branches to see whether I could keep from getting knocked out of the saddle, but after one or two of those it was fairly clear that he welcomed the outings, the chance to run, even with so poor a rider, and I became very attached to him. The jockey taught me how to groom the horses I rode. I was at home in the stable, which seemed to be an autonomous place, in those years. The jockey never noticed, or else paid no attention, when I borrowed a bridle from the tack room—which of course was locked when he left in the evening— and took it up to my room on the campus, so that I could come back down at night and slip it onto Bobby and ride out bareback, for hours, along the lanes through the woods, and across the open country.

One afternoon, out beside the lake, near a big stone house that stood by itself under the trees, a horse nickered and Bobby answered. A girl of my own age appeared on horseback. She lived in the stone house with her mother and brother. We became friends, and I rode out there often. The whole family was passionate about music, informed and opinionated. The girl with the horse sang—Bach arias. Her brother, back from traumatic active duty in the army in Europe, was an organist who wanted to be a composer, and with him Bach was an obsession. Bach, Bach, Bach —and I learned other names, of composers I had never heard of, and listened to records out there, on a stone terrace facing the lake.

Other friends from Princeton, all of them fellow waiters, took to coming out to the house by the lake and listening to music, and sitting talking in a kind of half secret retreat that we had found, and the girl, Nancy Merkel, and her mother, Charlotte, remained friends through my years at Princeton and afterward. But I was always there at that house with Bobby. He was the magic that had brought me, and that was something I had come to believe about him, wherever we went together. He made something possible that was ordinarily forbidden and unknown.

I learned more about music by simply listening to an obviously gifted and already learned fellow-student, Charles Rosen, who loved to talk about whatever figure—musical or literary—was his current obsession. He seemed equally brilliant about literature, both French and English, and music, and since his practice room, on the ground floor of the old art museum, was just across the grass from my room in the dormitory, I spent hours at my open window or lying out on the grass listening to him playing Scarlatti and—again—Bach, Bach. Twenty years after we had both left the university, at a big literary party in New York, Charles walked across the room and resumed a conversation exactly where we had left it off, all those years before. His memory for music, for literature, and clearly for whatever interested him, had always been phenomenal.

I signed up to sing in the choir (which earned me a few dollars) and learned a little about singing from Carl Weinrich, and I got to hear him play and rehearse on the chapel organ, Buxtehude, Mozart, and Bach, Bach.

Music, almost from the moment I arrived at Princeton, that summer of 1944, had come to occupy an important place in my life. I had no record player of my own, but there was one, with a shelf or two of classical records, in the upstairs sitting room of the Student Center, and since there were so few civilian students the room was usually empty. I would stop there, if I had time on my way between lectures and the dormitory, and listen to music. Suddenly I was overwhelmed by Beethoven. I played every record of his music in the collection there over and over. In the choir we began rehearsals of the Beethoven Mass in C Major, and in phrase after phrase I felt as though I were being led through some vast portico. I took out of the library books on Beethoven's life and the development of his music, and he became for me a hero, a reassuring and exemplary spirit, an embodiment of hope.

Two other such figures, during those first semesters at Princeton, were Milton and Shelley. No one had led me to expect the resounding splendor of Milton's language, its chthonic power. After a while I had most of the first book of *Paradise Lost* by heart, and I loved *Samson Agonistes* and some of the sonnets with the same fervent gratitude. Milton's Satan, via some suggestion found in a note, led me to Blake's Satan and to my first wandering exploration of Blake, and so to the Romantics, and Shelley, whose passion for freedom from the arrogations of authority—what Keats called his "poems about the deaths of kings"—probably appealed to me as much as his verse. That same ardor, which Shelley, and Blake's and Milton's Satan, and (it seemed to me) Milton and Beethoven shared, was a welcome, clarion note for me. They all nurtured an impulse that I had carried with me from childhood, from the days of my father's capricious strictures and punishments, which were in part intended—although I am sure he was not aware of it—to cripple me with his own besetting fears.

At that same time my reading, through byways that I have forgotten, led me to Spinoza, his *Ethics,* which seemed to elucidate and confirm things that I had been groping toward, among them a liberation from the religious fundamentalism in which I had been brought up.

The first modern poet I came to was Federico Garcia Lorca, whose poetry was an obsession of my Spanish teacher. And then William Arrowsmith, from the height of his few years of seniority and his irascible assurance, interrupted the Shelley that I was reading as I walked across the campus, by reading aloud Wallace Stevens's lines beginning

> *Bethou me, said sparrow, to the crackled blade,*
> *And you, and you, be thou me as you blow . . .*

and with that I was caught by something new, by modern poetry in English, by Stevens, and then by Eliot, and by Pound with his heartening insistence on the possibility of a provincial American being a poet.

For some reason, though I have no mathematical aptitude, a number of my student friends were mathematicians. Norman Hamilton, for example, who was physically shapeless as jelly and uncoordinated, but in his third semester as an undergraduate, was earning money by teaching math courses at the graduate school. He would talk about mathematics and I would talk about horses, and we must have understood something that way. I took him to the corral, and he gazed in amazement at these large incomprehensible creatures that I so admired. He was skeptical about everything, gentle, wholly impractical, and a wonder, like Rosen. It was strange to see Norman balancing a tray, an equation in wavering motion.

Another waiter friend, who was privately determined by then, as I was, to be a poet, was Galway Kinnell, and he was as footloose in his outlook. Both of us continued to wait on table all through our undergraduate years, but the head waiters clearly were never impressed by our attitudes or reliability, for we shared the distinction of being the only two waiters who had been on the job for so long without ever being promoted. Galway had a mentor, Charles Bell, a generation older than we were, who lived off campus and taught, without tenure, at the university, and talked of German literature and the arts of central Europe. Charles was deep in Goethe's *Elective Affinities,* and he became an intellectual father to Galway, and has remained so.

The two who came to occupy an analogous place in my life there were Richard Blackmur and John Berryman. Neither was there when I first arrived, but a few students who were hoping to be writers frequented a small bookstore that had opened in a house along Nassau Street, the Parnassus Bookshop, run by Keene and Anne Fleck, and it was Anne who told me about Blackmur, and about the proposed Creative Writing Program that was just getting started under his direction. Anne looked like a gypsy, and she had a remarkable sympathetic gift for sizing up character and originality. Again and again she pointed me toward people of interest who came and went in the two rooms of their bookshop. She suggested that I write to Blackmur and ask to be admitted to the writing course.

I met Blackmur and Berryman, who was to be his assistant, one rainy afternoon when those who had been accepted for the new program gathered to sign up for it. Blackmur was sitting calmly at a desk, his cigarette held, as usual, between his third and fourth fingers, his low, resonant, even voice sounding as though it was answering all questions with oracular authority in a few words. The rest of us, including John Berryman, were standing around in raincoats, John in a pork-pie hat. He stood in one spot, hollow-cheeked, seeming to revolve slowly as though he were suspended, his real attention apparently somewhere above our heads. He was responding to prospective students one by one, in his nasal, side-long, snapping tone, high-strung, with high-flown odds and ends of an English accent. The room smelled of wet rain-clothes and umbrellas. Berryman's contribution to the program, I came to realize, would be influenced by memories of his time in England, at Cambridge.

In the year or two that followed I would take my sheaf of bela-bored verses once a week up the narrow old stairs of the Pyne Building to John's small office, where he would unhesitatingly, mercilessly, reduce them to nothing, in the course of which I learned some extremely valuable things from him. I listened without resentment. For him poetry, as I heard him tell a group assembled one evening in the Parnassus Bookshop to listen to him read poems of Yeats and Hardy, was a matter of life and death. He cared about it more than he did about anyone's ego, including his

own, which made his caustic manner pardonable, and some of
the things he imparted to me lit up like discoveries of my own,
and never left me. His awareness of the importance of the order
of words and syntax, and of what he called movement in poetry
and its relation to the life, the charge of the language of verse, was
intense, unremitting, and fierce. It was part of the way he read
poetry, and it was a revelation to me. His own reading of English
poetry, and his memory of poems, were exhaustive, and much of
the poetry he had read seemed to be before him whenever he
spoke. He left me week after week with a cluster of new names in
my head to be tracked down in the library and pored over, trying
to find the fire in them.

Blackmur became an altogether different figure in my life. He
seemed much older, though he was only in his forties. In conversation, and in the series of long evening lectures that he gave in
Whig Clio Hall on Joyce, Flaubert, and Mann, I felt I was listening
to a literary intelligence of immense originality, authenticity, and
subtlety. The play and the horizons of his mind, his basic sense
that a critic, and so a reader, was a "house waiting to be haunted,"
were exhilarating, and particular insights of his about poetry and
literature remained with me as illuminations. I am sure he recognized and valued Berryman's creed of poetry as an absolute for
which nothing was ever adequate, but his nature turned it to the
light rather differently. Art, literature, the creations of the imagination, as he saw them, were inexhaustible, but not greater than
the whole of life that they represented. He was troubled, finally,
by his sense that Yeats and Mann, whom he admired passionately,
suggested that art, and the art of words, might be an end in itself,
greater than the life they came from. He might quote Saint Augus-
tine to the effect that the work of the imagination is an increment
to the divine creation, but he remained reassured by the thought
that "the best order [as I recall the sentence] is the higglety-
pigglety we know, but that we do not dare—only God does."

Sometimes his sentences, like that one, were knotty and enigmatic, which no doubt was the way he wanted them to be. In later years, those few whom I have met or read who were impatient with his talk or his writing have objected to the difficulty of some of what he said or wrote, assuming that his gnostic "obscurity" was deliberate and even perverse. I soon came to revere him, and it seemed to me that his idiosyncratic, intricate phrases conveyed perceptions whose complexity could not be presented in any other way, and that they required, indeed, a close and sympathetic —and patient—attention.

Richard Blackmur's awareness of me and of my own aspirations was something that I knew of, for the most part, indirectly and by chance, but I learned eventually that he had championed me when my own deviations as a student had aggravated some members of the faculty. I heard later, from a young professor, that at one faculty gathering he had asked a dean whether he had ever heard of Don so-and-so from Oxford. The dean said he had not. "Well, that's not surprising," Blackmur had said. "Almost the only thing he's remembered for now is that it was he who had Shelley thrown out of Oxford." Blackmur, more than anyone, was responsible for my remaining at Princeton, graduating, and going on to graduate school in Romance languages. "A good education," he said to me once, "won't do you any harm." And he, like Berryman, opened the work of writer after writer to me like a new country.

After my parents, those two, Berryman and, above all, Blackmur, probably had more to do with forming my outlook, by the time I left for Europe, than anyone I had known.

8

A number of my older friends, particularly the returning veterans, were married, some of them living in ramshackle one-room apartments off campus. On weekdays we tended to gather at the Student Center to pick up our mail and sit around talking while we read it. The idea of having a woman partner living in one's own room was a tantalizing notion. It would be years before Princeton admitted women as students, and there were very few young women around. One day when the subject of marriage came up I said, not seriously, that I supposed I would have to get married too, whereupon my friends turned on me as one, telling me that I was much too young for that. I had been told again and again that I was too young for something or other, and in a rush of impatience I said, "We'll see about that," and went out to the pay phone in the hall and called the Physics Department where Dorothy Ferry, my girlfriend at the time, was the secretary, and I proposed getting married.

Dorothy and I had met a few months before that. She had been walking across the campus with a friend, another secretary in the

Physics Department, and I was on my way across it with a student friend. In the days before women were admitted to Princeton as students, young feminine figures on the campus stood out like primary colors. My friend knew Dorothy's companion. We stopped to talk. Dorothy was pretty and pleasant and somehow I arranged to see her later, and we began to spend time together, on walks and then in my room.

Dorothy was living with her family in Morrisville, Pennsylvania, across the Delaware River from Trenton. It was a short bus ride from Princeton, and before long I went down with Dorothy and met her mother, Jenny, who worked as a travelling representative for Lerners Shops and between trips liked to spend her time at home. Dorothy's father, Daniel, turned up. He was a big, burly, red-faced second-generation Irishman who had been a Golden Gloves boxing champion, or so he claimed and we all believed it. He was also a fairly regular drinker, bad tempered when in his cups, and he went in for bouts of staggering drunkenness fairly regularly, at the end of which he usually managed to drag himself home through the back streets, though sometimes he rested in the gutter on the way, and occasionally he woke up with his wallet missing. And I met Dorothy's sister, Gloria, who had a job and a boyfriend but came home for weekends.

Jenny had come from a family of fervent Christian Scientists on Long Island and had found the pious atmosphere of her childhood so suffocating that she had sworn, in adolescence, that she would marry the first man who would take her away from there. By then she had a job in a Kushman's Bakery. Dan had come in one day, tall, young, stalwart, and handsome, and had fallen for her, and apparently she had fallen for him—at least she had fallen far enough so that when he proposed to her, in circumstances that neither of them mentioned, she had accepted, although his means of livelihood had not been discussed and they had had little by way of general conversation. Dan repeated that because he had met Jenny in a Kushman's Bakery he took off his hat every time he saw another shop in the chain, and they had had to leave Long Island because there were too many Kushman Bakeries there and he was catching cold.

The house was a tiny, low-ceilinged dwelling along the towpath of the derelict canal threaded behind the river towns between Philadelphia and Easton, a relic of the days before steam and rails. Jenny had found the house and bought it, and it was hers. The building may have been there before Washington crossed the Delaware, a few miles upriver. There were two small rooms in front, facing the small street, and a kitchen behind one of them, looking out toward the canal. A narrow boxed-in flight of stairs led up between the two front rooms, and another narrow, boxed-in flight led from the kitchen to the upstairs back bedroom. Small though it was, the house may have lodged two families in its early days. There had once been a big fireplace between the front rooms. The brick chimney was still part of the wall. But the fireplace was gone and had been replaced by a bulking kerosene stove, the only source of heat in the house.

The whole family, from Jenny to the aged police dog named Queenie, took me in at once, and Jenny and I got along like old friends. She loved books, had read widely all her life, and she was funny, irreverent, independent, and kind, with an adventurous streak that had helped her to make her own way to a life that she liked. There was still something between her and Daniel, though she made it clear that she was quite independent of him. But she was content to come home with him there, and share the back bedroom. She loved the house itself, and she kept Dan in his place, scolding him for his drinking, but giving him somewhere to hang his hat. He would have a few drinks, most evenings, on his way back from the foundry where he worked, and more if he had been out with the boys on a Saturday afternoon. He would open the door with a kind of lurch, and come in smelling of drink, and

Jenny would say, "Dan, you've been drinking," and he would deny it and sit down and pretend to read the paper. Later we would all sit at the round table in the kitchen and eat Jenny's goulash. He would have two heaping plates, eating with his face down over his dish, breathing hard, looking up grinning, and then he would push the plate away and say, "You know I hate goulash," and mean it. Sometimes after dinner we would play cards, usually Rummy, and sometimes we would cheat Dan, but in any case he usually lost, and when he did he would get angry and stomp up the stairs to the bedroom. The string to turn the light on up there hung in the middle of the room, and we would hear him stumbling against the furniture until he caught it.

Dan had come from a family that Jenny referred to as "shanty Irish," a couple of train stops down toward Philadelphia. She said that when she met Dan his family had never heard of any way of cooking potatoes except boiling them. Dan told stories about them, or made glancing references to them, and Jenny told versions that were more coherent. Dan's boxing career must have been a brief glory for them, and she had met Dan when he was still riding the wake of that wave. He boasted of Irish parties taking a whole trolley car to a beach park, with a washtub of beer on the front platform and one of the Ferry boys taking the tops off with his teeth. Dan's Irish-born father, often sustained by drink, had still stumbled along at a relatively advanced age, earning a living as a gandy dancer on the railroad, walking along the tracks with a sledge hammer, looking for spikes that had started to work loose out of ties, and whacking them back in with his maul. According to the account that had entered the family legend, the old man, as a result of fatigue or refreshment, had missed the spike with his mallet one day a few years back, and had brought the sledge down on his foot instead. He had lain writhing on the tracks for some time before he was found, and when they took him to the hospital he died on the operating table.

Shortly after I met Dan, someone at the foundry gave him a fireman's three-section extension ladder and had it delivered to the house. It was, Dan said, a very valuable ladder, and he leaned it up in front of the house, where even without being extended at all it rose above the roof toward the big trees that had grown tall along the canal. He climbed up and crept around the roof looking for damaged shingles, which he had never thought to do before that, and then he moved the ladder around to the back of the house and checked the other side, and cleaned out the gutters carefully, crawling along the edges, and then he came down and tried to decide what to do with the ladder.

He did not want to leave it leaning up against the house, of course, away up above the chimney, as though there was work going on there that hadn't been finished. He said it would be very useful if ever they needed to paint the house, but the house had been covered with white-enameled aluminum shingles, which he called alunium, and according to the guarantee it would never need to be painted. But he said the ladder would come in handy if they painted the upstairs window frames. If it was left leaning against the house, though, it would give burglars an idea about getting in that way.

So he laid the ladder down, three sections thick, across the front of the house, but burglars could see it there just the same, and it made it impossible to go in or out through the front door without stepping over it. Besides, Queenie, the old police dog who was so swaybacked that her belly nearly touched the ground, could not go in or out with it there. Burglars would be discouraged by how heavy it was, he said as he moved it around to the side of the house and laid it against the house there, but it was so long that it stuck out past the front and back corners, so that it was hard to walk around the house without falling over it. He moved it around to the back of the house and laid it to rest under the eaves, but then the back door could not be opened at all, and besides, Dan said, it would be too easy for someone to steal it from back there along the canal. For a while he considered laying it flat on the roof, but there was no way to fasten it up there, and what if it fell off in a high wind or something, and besides, once it was up there how could you get up there to take it down again if you wanted it?

He kept saying what a valuable ladder it was, though, and finally after days and weeks of deliberation and unsuccess he was visited by an idea, and opened one of the windows in the back bedroom, where Jenny and he slept, heaved the ladder up over the window frame, with some wear and tear on the sill, and went up inside the house, opened the door between the back room and the one in front of it, and dragged the ladder through. If it was angled right the ladder occupied the floor all the way from the front wall to the back window, where it stuck out toward the canal, but well out of reach of burglars. It was not ideal, but he felt it was a solution and believed he could angle it better so that it would lie on the floor and the window could close. He finally managed that, by moving the bed farther across the room into the corner, and running the ladder at a smart rake through the doorway.

But after that, in the evenings when he had lost at cards again and stormed up the back stairs to the bedroom, we would sit waiting, listening for him to find the string for the light, out in the middle of the room, and once the ladder was in place up there we could count the footsteps until we heard a terrible crash as he fell over the ladder in the dark. It happened regularly until one night we heard him limp cautiously back down the stairs, until he stood at the foot staring at us and said, "God damned booby trap." And to Jennie he said, "Dearie, that ladder. It's a valuable piece of equipment if we ever need it. I won't lend it to nobody. I won't give it away. I won't sell it to nobody. I got nowhere to put it. I *hate* it." Then he went back up the stairs cautiously as though he hoped to get past it without waking it.

His drinking habits got worse during Jennie's trips away for Lerner's, which he resented but grudgingly accepted because he knew he had to. The ladder too may have weighed on his mind. One morning after Dan had been out late, Jenny came downstairs early and found a pool of vomit inside the front door, on the carpet. She waited for Dan to come down, and confronted him with it. "Dan, you were drunk last night. Look at that. It's disgusting."

Dan said, "Queenie done it."

Jenny said, "Are those Queenie's teeth in the middle of it?"

The household certainly was unlike any other that I had ever been part of, though it recalled houses of school friends of mine where I had been welcome as a child, in which I had never been allowed to spend as much time as I would have liked. There had been several families who lived up the back alley behind our house in Scranton, for instance. Billy Mulligan's, with his friendly, good-humored father who occasionally was seen coming home on his hands and knees, and his happy, retarded sister, Mary. And the Genoveses, the sexton's family with their Italian doughnuts and their sewing machines in every room, which they taught me to use. Jenny had escaped to this backyard from the stifling respectability of Long Island, and her parents seemed to relish the life she had made for herself, to take a kind of vicarious pleasure in her escape, whatever they may have made of Dan. Jenny was the free-wheeling soul of the house into which I was adopted without raising a ripple, and where I was taken for granted. Gloria, too, came and went with her boyfriend. There was no talk about plans, and I still had none when I went out to telephone Dorothy, two hundred yards away in the Physics Department, to suggest that we get married.

Dorothy was agreeable, equable, and attractive. She was a little older than I was, and had had one affair, for several years, with an older man. She liked to treat herself, several times a year, to trips to New York, with a woman friend, to the ballet, and her room was hung with reproductions of Degas paintings. To me, surrounded by married friends, having a regular girlfriend, on a campus where young women were rarely seen, seemed a slightly improbable, pleasantly disreputable gift of fortune. When I proposed marriage, on the phone, she accepted, as though I had suggested going out for lunch, and I went back in and told the boys, and for once enjoyed their fussing about my youth. When I told my mother, she too, tried to discourage the idea, but when I spoke to my father, fresh out of his chaplain's uniform, and the army, and asked him to marry us, he came and performed the ceremony, before a few witnesses, in the huge empty Gothic Princeton chapel, although he surely had his misgivings too.

✳ ✳ ✳

By the time I met Alain Prévost, some four years after his father's death, I had graduated, defiantly wearing a small beard like Ezra Pound's (and then shaved it off). The uniforms had almost all gone from the Princeton campus by then, and the civilian students, including returning veterans, were filling it again. Dorothy and I were living in a single room on Bank Street, a one-block dead end, and we soon moved into the newly built Harrison Street Project, a development of small houses for married students, built from army barrack sections and arranged like an army base on the overgrown pastures where Bobby and I had ridden a few years before. The eating clubs were open again, and the social stratifications of Princeton social life had also returned, yet all of that seemed to be behind me. But Alain, as I came to know him, was a tenuous link to the traditional country-club Princeton of the twenties, the era of raccoon coats and Stutz Bearcats, of F. Scott Fitzgerald's side of paradise, which had formed in Alain's mind before he ever left

France, and which was represented for him, and in part for me, by what he knew of Alan Stuyvesant and Alan's older brother Louis. It was Alan Stuyvesant who had brought Jean Prévost's son Alain to the States after the war and managed to enroll him at Princeton. I am not sure where Alain and I met. Probably it was at a party, something connected with the French Department. The Department itself had such gatherings from time to time, and so did Maurice Coindreau, who was busy translating and introducing American writers such as Faulkner and Carson McCullers to France, and there were parties on the occasions of Robert Casadessus's piano concerts. I went to those parties with an abiding sense of my inadequacy in French. Whatever I knew of the language I had acquired during the summer of 1947 in a crash course at McGill University in Montreal. I felt a similar inadequacy in Spanish, despite years of classroom study, as I listened to the nuanced, elegant, precise Castillian of Americo Castro's lectures on Cervantes' *Novelas Ejemplares*. In both languages, in which I was supposedly at ease, I kept struggling to catch up, to grasp the tail of the phrase, the syllable, the intonation, the implication that had just escaped me. I knew I was going about it the hard way, trying to catch the lost music of Villon and of the *coplas* of Jorge Manrique. Alain was trying to exercise his English, which he had learned in classrooms and out of books, but it was still like a pebble in his mouth. I remember that I liked him immediately: his frank good humor, his lack of self-importance, his unabashed interest in the world around him, combined with a curious, abiding (he probably would have been happy, at that point, to call it "Gallic") skepticism. To him life seemed to be an outing. We became friends at once, recognizing some shared, uncanonical appetite for existence.

Alain was a couple of years younger than I was, as I learned eventually. I never noticed the difference in age between us. It was clouded by his newcomer's comparative strangeness to everything around him, something he tried to disguise and to use to his advantage, and his European upbringing and background gave him a range of reference that allowed him to seem more worldly-wise than many of the students around him, and in fact more sophisticated than he really was. But his newness in the New World, at Princeton, and his open nature, gave him a constant impulse to explore, to examine, to take in, a boyish eagerness that I recognized. We formed an adventurous friendship of a kind I had not been able to have as a child. I was a good audience for his tales of his French childhood in Normandy, which sounded exotic and enchanted to me. I imagined them set in a landscape configured by Alain-Fournier's *Le Grand Meaulnes*. We shared many likes and dislikes, from behavior to music. With the coming of spring in 1948 we took to making relatively impromptu hitch-hiking trips to spots on the Jersey shore, sleeping under boardwalks or on benches, and walking along back roads.

The wartime three-semester-a-year schedule at the university had ended, and summer was coming. Alain had told me of Alan Stuyvesant's bringing him to America in fulfillment of his promise to Jean Prévost, and one day he informed me, with some excitement, that this avuncular eminence in his life was looking for a tutor for his nephew Peter, who had lost a year's school as a result of rheumatic fever. Alain said he would suggest me for the job if I was interested, and Alan Stuyvesant drove down to Princeton one day to look me over.

9

Alan arrived in a new brown Jeep station wagon, a model that had been developed in the wake of the jeep's World War II legend. It had a wicker-work pattern on the sides, a lot of room, space in back for dogs—as I learned—and anything else. Alan raised Brittany spaniels, for field and show, and his own favorite, Chesta, was with him.

One day near the end of that summer Alan would confess quietly and ruefully to having arrived at his forty-seventh birthday. He was round-faced, with red veins on his cheeks and a brush of dark moustache, and little hair left on top of his head. Medium height, slightly overweight, rounded in the middle and on the way to becoming portly. He walked with a flat-footed, knock-kneed gait, rocking from side to side when he was in a hurry, like a metronome or a wooden figure of the Little King wobbling down an incline. Though he displayed little physical grace he was someone of decisive energy, affable in manner but watchful and determined. Someone who was used to having his own way and being in charge. He surveyed Princeton with a seasoned familiarity, a disenchanted fondness, like a former owner who knew the present owners but seldom saw them. He was brisk, but he seemed to have grown into his elder role quite naturally.

Alan had told Alain that he was afraid I might be too young for the job. I was twenty. And there was another young man whom Alan was considering, whom he had already met and had arranged to see there again. The other candidate, an athletic, clean-cut student of twenty-three, showed up before long, and a rather awkward conversation—or semblance of it—began. We did not manage to discover the slightest interest in common. Alan and he walked aside for a few minutes, and then Alan came back and drove down to the housing project with me to meet Dorothy and see where and how we lived, and then to take us to his own domain.

On the way up through the suburbs of central New Jersey Alan told Dorothy and me a little about his family relationship to Peter. Peter's father, Louis, had been Alan's older brother, and as Alan told it, Louis had always been the star. He had been handsome, athletic, and dashing, a better boxer—they had both been boxers —and a drinker and playboy. He and Alan had had twin foreign sports cars, and they used to race them, sometimes in inappropriate places, and not always when they were sober. Once they had set out from a party, on a bet, and raced to the Mexican border. Alan's accounts, however they may have been magnified by the passage of time, obviously alluded to a Great Gatsby Princeton rather than the relatively toned-down scene of my own experience, in which I knew of no students who had cars. (Students were not allowed to keep cars on campus.) Louis, Alan told us, had been divorced from Peter's mother. There were two children. Peter had an older sister, Diana. Louis had died—as a result, it seemed from the way Alan told it, of his drinking. That was a few years back, and Alan was trying to help with the children, as well as he could.

We pulled up outside a small new ranch-type house on a semicircular suburban street, in a development where all the trees were guyed to stakes and appeared to be about two years old. I have no idea why Alan's sister-in-law, Louis's divorced widow, had picked that place to live, and it was not the moment to ask. Peter and his mother and sister were expecting us. We all stood in the small, new living room cluttered like a children's playroom, while Alan and Peter's mother talked past each other. Peter was a thin, pleasant, evidently shy boy with brush hair growing out and big braces on his teeth. He seemed uncertain, watchful, and likeable. His sister was quiet too, taller, graceful, and watchful too, like a herd dog around sheep that were not hers, unwilling to be drawn into the talk at all, but not wanting to miss anything that was said. Their mother seemed to have grown into a middle-age of unadorned resentment, or at least that was the aspect of herself that she preferred to present to Alan and anyone who might be with him. She was small, thin, perhaps athletic, with cropped hair and no makeup. She made no pretense of being glad to see anyone, and no one was invited to sit down. After a few exchanges, jollied along by Alan, he suggested that Dorothy and I go out and talk with Peter while he stayed inside to discuss things with Peter's mother.

Out behind the car, Peter too was reticent and cautious, but without hostility. Instead of asking him, yet, about himself, I asked him what he wanted to do that summer, and he began to answer, in monosyllables at first, about wanting to spend it at Alan's Deer Park house, out west of Hackettstown, a place that Peter obviously loved. He was telling us about the place when Alan came back out, looking blank, spoke affectionately to Peter for a moment, and then said he would see him soon, and he and Dorothy and I drove off.

He told us as we went that he had never managed to like Peter's mother very much, though she had been lively, original, and unrecognizably different when she was younger and she and Louis were first running around together. It had been a stormy affair from the start, and the marriage had grown stormier, as everyone had been able to see. The atmosphere of the storms became chronic. Louis's drinking and—Alan suggested—his playing around made it worse, whatever she herself may have done to contribute to it. He said that the divorce was finally triggered, as both she and Louis told it in different ways, when one day, in the course of one of their bouts of mutual recrimination, she had turned her back and bent to pick up something from the floor, and while her behind was facing him his hand fell on a toy bow and target arrow with a rubber suction cap on the end. Later there was some question as to whether or not he had been sober or drunk, but either way he had shot her in the seat and that was that. To Alan it seemed to epitomize their whole story. No doubt he was telling us about it because of his own immediate annoyance with her and the way she had received us all, but I wondered whether his revelation of this unedifying nugget of family history, a critical moment so close to him, might be an indication that he had made up his mind to offer me the job as Peter's tutor. I had no idea, then or later, whether he ever brought the other prospective candidate to meet Peter and his mother. He must have been pondering the choice ever since Alain had first proposed me, on the basis of whatever Alain told him. Alain said to me later that the fact that I was married and seemed to have settled down a bit had been important in his choosing me. And it seems likely that his old loyalty to Jean Prévost, relayed via Alain, extended to a leaning in favor of Alain's new friends.

Before Alan let himself out of her front door, he and Peter's mother must have agreed that Peter would spend the summer at the Deer Park, and no doubt that Alan would pick a tutor she could accept, so that Peter could make up the studies he had missed.

10

Dorothy kept her good job at Princeton, as the head secretary of the Physics Department and of Harold Smyth, its chairman. Prof. Smyth had worked on the atomic bomb at Los Alamos and had written the first lay reader's guide to the subject, *Atomic Physics*. As soon as the news of the bomb broke, ordinary students like me began to learn of the connections of the Princeton Physics and Mathematics departments, and of figures around Princeton from Alfred Einstein to Robert Oppenheimer, with the evolution of the project. Dorothy worked at Princeton during the week, so it was on a weekend that Alan came to take us to the Deer Park the first time. On this trip he had Peter with him.

Peter was excited to be on his way to the Deer Park, which all his life had been one of his favorite places. He kept asking Alan about things there, about the dogs, and the lake, and the elk, and Alan filled in around his answers so that we understood more or less what they were talking about. I thought Peter might be relieved, besides, to be getting away from his mother, and to be on his way to a part of his life where she would not follow him or hear what he said. By the time we got to Hackettstown Peter was telling us what we would see next, and the elation of his homecoming affected all of us.

When I last saw Hackettstown, more than twenty years ago, the middle of town had not changed much since those days. It still had the appearance of a country town, with frame buildings painted yellow or brown or green, a hardware store, and an old shingled hotel from the turn of the century, complete with rockers on the porches, on the main street near the central intersection. That first time, as we got to the center we stopped, and Alan and Peter went into the hardware store as though they were visiting an old friend, and picked up a few odds and ends, including fishing lures for Peter. Then we headed out through the west side of town, past a grain elevator and feed store by the railroad tracks, and over the tracks and up the hill.

From there on virtually everything that I remember of the place in those first summers has been wiped out, replaced by a veining of multilane highways, with the farmlands and woods graded out of existence to make way for a resort and shopping complex called Panther Valley (now that there are no more panthers), dreamed up in some cloned room miles away on a ninety-fifth floor. If the countryside I remember had to endure change, there is a certain relief in its having happened that way. It was not chewed at, dollied up, debased feature by feature, like so many remembered places, until it was unrecognizable and shameful before it was completely gone. Instead it has vanished altogether like an image on a screen, and when I see it now it is intact and untouchable.

We crossed the tracks and drove up the long hill toward Allamuchy. Already, on the way, Peter had managed to endow the name with a ring of legend. It was where the mail arrived for the Deer Park house: there was a post office box in the country store, which stood, among a few other unpainted wooden buildings, down a steep hill on a back road. The newspapers came there too, and the morning gossip for miles around.

But we were going to the Deer Park first. At the top of the hill we turned off to the right, along an unmarked dirt road. We reached a wire gate and closed it behind us. "We're here," Peter said. We were on land that had been in Alan's family since before the English drove the Dutch from power in the seventeenth century. The road led into mixed woods, under big trees, curved sharply left at what may once have been the corner of a field or a farm, passed a couple of big yellow frame farmhouses sitting among old trees on the right, and dropped to an open space with a row of fifteen or twenty kennels and runs behind chain-link fencing, and another farmhouse on the slope behind them. In a number of the runs Brittany spaniels were barking through the fences. There must have been a dozen dogs. Peter said sadly that there used to be more when Alan had more time for them. When Alan pulled up near the kennels a man in jeans and a checked shirt came around the side of a shed at the end of the runs and walked toward us, smiling. He was Harold Franz, who took care of the dogs and, as we soon came to understand, a great deal else at the Deer Park. In most respects he was in charge of the place. Peter was clearly delighted to see him and to ask him about the dogs. Alan and Peter and Harold went off to the kennels, deep in discussion, and came back in a few minutes with Alan's dark Brittany, Chesta, and a bigger, younger dog, Beth, who was Peter's, at least when Peter was at the Deer Park. While they were catching up on practical matters, Alan remembered to make the introductions.

Harold was an agreeable man, obviously extremely capable and reliable, with a quiet authority. Alan said he had been there for some fifteen years. He and his wife and family lived in one of the farmhouses overlooking the kennels. The other houses there Alan used for guests, or occasionally rented out to friends. Harold and Alan went on conferring about the place, about dates for dog shows, painting to be done, tree work, fence work, plumbing repairs after the winter, messages from people in town. The dogs were loaded into the back of the station wagon. Then we drove over to the entrance of the Deer Park itself, a tall ranch gate, the side posts and top beam made of rough logs. Harold walked over with us to open the gate in the eight-foot-high fence. There was a chain and padlock on it, hanging unlocked, and another lock, Peter explained, was connected to Harold's house by an electric cable. You could call up Harold from a phone there on the gate-post, for him to let you in if he knew you. When we had driven through and Harold let go, a big cement weight on a wire cable descended behind us and closed the gate again. Keeping the deer in, Alan said, for they could jump anything up to eight feet, and in fact could go higher than that if they were frightened. And strangers out, he added, though he explained that he let local groups in for picnics and visits. The Rod and Gun Club came, and the Rotary Club, for fishing parties and to shoot ducks in season, and the Boy Scouts and Audubon Society had hikes and meetings and bird watching parties there.

We drove on into the woods for a mile, perhaps. The road was rutted, pot-holed, dotted with rocks and tree roots. Some of the trees appeared to be remnants of old forest—oaks, maples, beeches, tulip trees—Alan said he had no idea how ancient they might be. There were trunks three and four feet in diameter. The tops formed a high canopy over us. Then an open clearing on the right, gray snags standing at the edge of a wide marsh, a shallow basin, with more forest on the far side. It could have been part of the landscape that the first Europeans saw there, and that the tribes had known as the world, before that. Up a small hill, and we came to a stop across from a bit of gray board fence. Half hidden behind it was the roof of the Deer Park house, set down into the hillside so that it faced out over the marsh and the open valley.

Alan reminded me that he was an architect by profession, and he said part of the building appeared to be a house, or perhaps half house half barn, dating from long before the Revolution. Early eighteenth century, or even perhaps as early as the original European settlement around there. We carried our bags through the gate and down stone stairs to a walk along the back of the house. We could see below us that the lower floor of the house was built of dressed fieldstone, the dark masonry plain, elegant, and beautiful. The upper floor, which may have been added at a later date, was of wood: a broad clapboard painted a pale gray, almost white. The stone stairs turned to lead down to the ground level, but we went along the uphill side and into a back door to the upper floor, with the dogs tumbling in beside us. Alan showed us the bedrooms — cupped planks in the wavy, varnished floors, some of the windows set low in the walls, framed as though they were in boxes. Those were the old ones, Alan explained. The larger ones, set higher up, had been put in when the roof was raised at a much later date.

Downstairs he showed us the rest of the house. On the ground floor the ceilings were low, and so were the doorways between the rooms. Some of the walls were faced with broad, sawn, blue-painted boards. At one end, near the stairs, was the big kitchen, with a stone floor. That part of the house may have been a dairy or a barn, originally. At the other end was the wide living room with a broad stone fireplace taking up much of the far wall. A small plank door to the right of the fireplace opened onto stairs leading down and outside through a miniature cellar piled with firewood. From the kitchen, French doors, glazed with small panes, led out onto a wide stone terrace overlooking the open marshland and its wide green radiance. Those, and some of the other windows and later renovations, and the present roof, Alan admitted with a certain reticence, were of his own devising, but he had not wanted to alter the building in any essential respect. Besides the fact that he had grown up knowing it, he was obviously keenly aware of how beautiful it was, with its rooted plainness and the unremembered lives it had harbored.

In the kitchen Alan introduced us to Mary, a handsome, self-possessed, grown-up woman (the accepted word at the time was "colored") from Aiken, South Carolina, where Alan's family had kept a winter residence for several generations. She came up from Aiken in the spring, Alan explained to us while she stood there, to be the cook and housekeeper at the Deer Park house through the summer, and to keep things in line, as she had done ever since he was a child. Alan asked after her family in Aiken, and was asking her where Handy was when a colored man who must have been roughly Alan's own age appeared in the terrace door. It was Handy himself, the chauffeur and caretaker of the house, who started by apologizing for not having been there when Alan arrived, explaining that he had just been in to town and had got back, in the jeep, after we came. He too was from Aiken, and had followed the same schedule for many years. We stood in the kitchen for a moment, all together, and they alluded to the past and talked of the unknown summer ahead of us.

11

Mary had planned lunch on the terrace, and she set it out for us. "She is," Alan said, well within her hearing as she came and went, "a great cook," and Mary tossed her head as she went through the door, and raised her hand as though shooing a fly. The dogs lay on the stone near the door, watching both ways.

Peter wanted to go down to the lake right away, that afternoon, and as soon as lunch was over he started getting his fishing tackle ready, fetching his tackle box out of a closet, *his* closet, and sorting out the redolent contents on his bedspread. "We can change down there," Alan said. The jeep was parked by the station wagon, over toward a small, reed-bordered frog pond.

As we started up the stairs to the outside fence Chesta and Beth shot past us, Chesta in the lead, and raced around the cars to the reeds, slowing to prowl along the water's edge, heads down. "Chesta's after frogs," Alan said. "She never stops. She's so good at it, she gets too many of them." He led me up closer to the pond, walking cautiously. "Watch," he said, showing her off.

Chesta crept closer to the water, behind a tuft of reeds. "There's a frog there, in the reeds," Alan said in a low voice. Chesta made a short lunge, a feint, to the left side of the clump, flushing the frog so that it leapt to the right, just as she had known it would, and as it jumped she wheeled, pivoting on her left front paw, and leapt to the right, catching the frog in mid-air and tossing it over her shoulder onto the bank. "Come on, Chesta," Alan said, and Chesta looked up, undecided for a moment, perhaps hoping to bring the frog along, and then came over and jumped into the station wagon. With the toe of his shoe Alan flipped the live frog back into the water.

As Alan and Peter were shutting the dogs into the back of the station wagon, Alan turned to me and nodded toward the jeep, an army issue vehicle bought at a surplus outlet after the war. He'd asked whether I knew how to drive. I did not, and as a child had been forbidden, as from On High, ever to touch the controls of any machine. I was going to have to learn to drive if I was to spend the summer up there. "You can learn on the jeep," Alan said, "and practice on the roads in the park." They were jeep roads, certainly, as we saw on the mile or so between the Deer Park house and the first glimpse of the lake through big trees. Alan nursed the high-slung but more vulnerable station wagon along over boulders and across mud holes, around an appendage of the lake covered with water lilies, then through muddy ruts, past a marsh under big trees. A duck with a string of ducklings behind her paraded out of the marsh and crossed the ruts ahead of us, disappearing under the big leaves of skunk cabbage on her way to the lake.

"I hope they escape the snapping turtles," Alan said.

"Harold got a fifty pound one," Peter said with pride.

"And the hawks get some," Alan said. "There were golden eagles in there a few years ago," he added, "when my brother was here. My brother saw them first. And they took their share, I'm afraid. First nobody could believe they were golden eagles. The Audubon people came out and saw them and confirmed that that was what they were. Then the Rod and Gun people wanted to shoot them, because of the ducks, they said. We wouldn't let them do that. That's just what you have to expect if you have eagles, the price you have to pay. The cats take more than the eagles ever did. People from all around here dump cats up along the road, whole litters of them, and they come into the woods and go wild."

The road climbed to a low bank along the lake, running under tree limbs, with huge dead trunks sloping down into the water, and dark rocks the size of rooms along the shore.

"Turtles," Peter said, pointing along a mossy trunk almost covered with water. Four domes the size of small skulls, gray shells gleaming like old pewter, were lined up along the log, catching the sun.

"Not snappers, those," Alan said. We eased ahead past them on the road that skirted the lake, and came finally to a clearing, and a cabin set back from the shoreline, with a small porch across the front of it facing out toward the water. Dark board siding, a big stone chimney emerging from the middle of the roof, the whole of it set low to the ground. It looked like an Appalachian cabin in the southern mountains, and it occurred to me later that its form might have been suggested by buildings that the family knew well, near Aiken.

Alan parked on the slope behind the cabin and handed Peter the key to the front door, and Peter let us in. We stepped straight into a room with an oval table in the middle of the floor, and not much else except the broad stone fireplace. A heavy smell of squirrels, chipmunks, and bats rushed around us. Every surface appeared to be deep in dust and grit. There were nutshells on the floorboards and on the table, as we could see even in the gray darkness before Alan opened the shutters, front and back, and a back door into a small screened and shuttered kitchen. The fireplace rose like a rock spire through the middle of the building. On the far side of it was the other room, with a bed in it, the spring bare: they did not leave a mattress down there through the winter for the cabin's regular residents to nest in.

"You can change in there," Alan said to Dorothy. He and Peter went back out and we met on the porch a few minutes later in bathing suits.

"Harold put in the dock last week," Alan said to Peter. There was an orange canoe overturned on the end of it, and a float out in the water some eighty or ninety feet beyond it. From the front door of the cabin we had a broad view of the lake, looking bigger than it really was, shaped like a piece of a picture puzzle, with long arms extending back into the woods, out of sight. The dogs had been in the water already, and they stayed watching us until we came out, and then nosed off along the shore picking up scents, looking back toward us, heading out again, finally settling down beside us, in the sun.

12

When we got back to the house, Alan gave me my first driving lesson on the jeep. Gear positions. The importance of neutral.
Brakes. Ignition. Then the first spine-jolting stalls, with my foot
on the clutch pedal. Over and over, lurching and losing it, starting
up again in neutral, hand on the knob of the long rod vibrating in
the floor beside me. Finally getting it into gear once and leaping
forward at a speed that immediately felt out of control, finding
the brake pedal and stalling again, a few feet along the track. Alan
said little except, "Try again," but I sensed his impatience and certainly found it understandable. I had come to recognize, by then,
his chronic irritation with what he referred to as "intellectuals,"
and I was trying to figure out just what the term meant to him,
what trait or behavior it was that he found so annoying.

It may have been a residue of some moment in his own college
days when he felt exposed and vulnerable, and was sure that he
was looked down on by students and faculty members who knew
more than he did and were not impressed by the advantages that
he had always taken for granted. His aggravation was directed,

above all, at "intellectuals" in the humanities, and most specifically literature. He spoke of most writers of all kinds with a fixed condescension. The chief exceptions seemed to be F. Scott Fitzgerald and Hemingway, whom he clearly admired. He referred to Alain's mother—Jean Prévost's first wife, Marcelle Auclair, a very Catholic writer, author of a well-known (in French) biography of St. Theresa of Avila, and of a life of Federico Garcia Lorca—with a weary annoyance, suggesting that apart from her subjects she knew nothing worth knowing. But his exasperation did not seem to include Jean Prévost himself, a French literary "intellectual" by any definition. He always spoke of Jean with respect.

I encountered this uneasy prejudice of Alan's at the beginning, when he inquired about my graduate studies in French and learned that my enthusiasms were François Villon and the poets of the Pléiade, whom Alan dismissed, saying that he had had enough of them at school. From then on he described my French, to me and to others, as bookish (which was one of the least of its shortcomings) and obsolete. In fact it was merely student French, inexperienced and clumsy. My first attempts at driving the jeep, repeatedly fumbling his instructions, confirmed his prejudice that "intellectuals" were useless in the real world. Yet he had somehow decided that I would do, in the circumstances, and he even showed a kind of avuncular concern, as though I were a younger member of his family whom he was trying to shape up.

I managed to get the jeep into reverse, and stall and lurch back to the starting point without breaking our necks or demolishing anything, and Alan got out, saying that the Deer Park was about as safe a place for practicing as anyone could hope for, and suggesting that, with Handy's help, even I might be able to learn to drive there.

13

Alan took Dorothy back to Princeton the next day, Sunday, so that she would be ready for her job on Monday morning, and then he went on to wherever he was going. He told us nothing about his own plans, or the rest of his life. He had an apartment in New York, a top floor on Fifth Avenue across from the Metropolitan Museum, as I learned later, but I had no sense of what his life might be like away from the Deer Park.

His manner with Dorothy was amiable, polite, and without interest. She would stay in Princeton through the week while I was up at the Deer Park with Peter. She was welcome at the Deer Park on weekends, which was a further reason for my learning to drive. In the first days there with Peter I started to practice, after we had had our morning lessons and Mary had given us lunch.

Peter watched my uncoordinated controversy with the clutch with earnest attention and bouts of helpless hilarity, as though we were making up a new and not entirely permissible game. In spite of the awful jolts and sudden stops, after a while he climbed in, treating it like a dodgem ride at the county fair. Yet he himself took surprisingly little interest in the mechanical manipulations that I was trying to master, and was quite content to leave all that to me. My struggles with reverse gear, as I tried to keep the jeep running in a straight line backwards, without hitting anything, amused him—as they worried me—most. Handy, who must have heard the jeep's agonized arpeggios and winded grunts, came up to see if he could make things a little easier for the unfortunate machine. He gave me a few tips about the pedals, and then wisely instructed both of us on how to take off a wheel with the jack and wrench, and put on the spare, in case we had a flat—or something. His kindness, and my anxiety about the vehicle, were both magnified by the fact that the jeep was what he used himself for his trips to town almost every day. It must have been like his own wheel and freedom, and teaching me rudimentary repairs to it probably was a kind of protective gesture toward it. His manners in sharing it, that summer, were a model of grace. If he planned to be in town for any length of time he would come to find me, if he could, and tell me how long he expected to be using the jeep, "if it won't disconvenience you none." And whenever I asked, he would come and give me tips on my driving practice, always with unruffled patience. His lessons did not seem like lessons at all, but like private information that he wanted to pass on to me.

I was still far from mastering the reverse gear—in particular— when, after a few days of practice, Peter and I loaded fishing rods and tackle into the back of the jeep and set out for the lake. Peter regarded my stalling as a joke that got better the more often it was told, and he thought it was almost as funny if we hit a pothole or a root, or if I braked too hard on a tight corner. We could have walked to the lake, I think, in the time it took us to cough and bump our way there in the helpless jeep, and when we reached the cabin Peter got out and watched, convulsed, as I set about backing up on the slope and turning around to face the way we had come.

We had a swim, and then took out the canoe and trolled for

bass down near the lily pads, and Peter had a few bites that got away, and caught a couple of sunfish that were too small to keep.

Handy had given us the key to the cabin, which he kept in the kitchen, and we opened the building like a present, inspecting the darkness, the smell of wood and rodents, the dark pile of bat guano near the fireplace. We talked about whether the bats would be driven out, as Peter said they had been sometimes, or would be left alone, which was what he wanted. He was fascinated by wild creatures of every kind. His father and Alan had been white hunters in Africa. There were skins of lions and tigers, and beautiful rippled horns of hoofed creatures on the walls and floors in the Deer Park house, and Alan had told me that they had met Hemingway and had heard local gossip about Isak Dinesen—another writer he approved of, and whose books Peter and I talked about, that summer. But although he loved to fish, Peter had no interest in the killing of animals. The bats intrigued him. He wanted to watch them, to learn about them, not to intrude upon them. He was interested in the turtles —there were several kinds in the park—and in the frogs and toads and water newts and all the different species of snakes that lived around us. It was the natural, quite ordinary interest of a boy of his age, but in him it was remarkably gentle, and seemed to represent some cherished, sequestered hope. We found on the shelves in the house Ditmars' *Reptiles of North America,* and we both pored over it, using it as a reference to identify whatever reptiles we encountered, and talking about the text and about Ditmars himself, who had died from the bite of a rattlesnake—a hatchling, scarcely as long as his thumb, that he was moving from one aquarium tank to a larger one. The infant snakes had been so small that he had not worn gloves, and one of them had sunk its needle fangs into his hand as he picked it up. Because of the creature's size he thought he did not need to attend to the bite until he had finished transferring them all, and by the time he did so the venom had been carried along his bloodstream to his heart, and it was too late to save him. The moral, as the note in the posthumous edition emphasized, was that the poison of pit vipers was the same poison at any age. The hatchlings' fangs were little and fine and the actual quantity of poison they could inject was slight, but it could still be fatal if you did nothing about it.

Peter and I found other books about animals and old copies of *National Geographic* in the house, and passed them back and forth. During the summer we built a dam across the small stream that wound into the marsh, below the Deer Park house, and we watched the pond life colonize it: water striders, dragonflies, other water insects, small water snakes, more turtles, newts, salamanders. We acquired several aquariums of different sizes, for indoors and out. Peter caught a small water snake and a turtle, and kept them in one of the smaller glass tanks. He wanted to keep that one out of the way of Mary's attention, and he took to changing the water in his own bathtub. Inevitably, the water snake escaped and disappeared down the drain. We gave it up. Then a few hours later, when the aquarium had been hidden somewhere else, the snake emerged from the air vent in the washbasin in Peter's bathroom, and he caught it again.

The assortment of amphibians and reptiles in the aquariums grew. Mary tried to ignore them. The most prized captive among them was a harmless hognose snake, popularly known as a puff adder—a misleading nickname, for the real puff adder is a deadly snake from Africa. Our hognose snake was about eight inches long, and at first, when it was disturbed, it tried to act dangerous by hissing and swelling and rearing up, but after a few days it grew accustomed to our taking the glass lid off the aquarium and cleaning out the inside, and it paid little attention to us unless we startled it. We even got to where we could pick it up gently and it would lie still in our hands. Snakes are said to like the warmth of touch. But we made a rule, for the collections, not to keep anything in captivity for more than ten days, and though Peter broke the rule, occasionally, for favorites, he never kept them for much longer than that. We knew that in the long run we could not provide them with what they needed, and that they were bound to suffer, and perhaps not survive, as a result.

We collected butterflies too, and kept them in jars with perforated lids, along with the leaves of plants and trees that the books said they lived on. They were kept for a day or two at most, to see whether they would lay eggs on the leaves. Sometimes they did not survive even that long in the jars. The books on butterflies that we had available did not seem as helpful as the ones on reptiles and amphibia. Neither of us had any wish to kill them for mounted collections, and in fact our interest in butterflies was haphazard and absentminded.

But the fascination with animal life that Peter and I shared was a thread running through our days, occurring in the course of our studies in the morning, leading us out to the aquariums and the dam before and after lunch. It was a strand in the new affinity that emerged between us, spontaneous, not competitive, slightly conspiratorial, unnamed. Surely it was an element of friendship, and for me it must have fulfilled something that I had wanted and had not been allowed to pursue or develop when I was younger, except in brief, exceptional, disconnected moments, inevitably interrupted if the playing became noisy and "overheated." Within a few days it seemed as though in Peter I had acquired a younger brother, and in many of the things we did together—the lake, the dam, the books we both read, the drives in the jeep—the difference in our ages became increasingly unimportant.

14

We drove to the lake every afternoon, with the driving growing less bucked and choppy, my use of the clutch and accelerator and brake gradually coming to be surer and smoother, and we began to explore the "roads"—the rutted wagon tracks leading past the cabin into the rest of the Deer Park. One such track went all the way around the five-thousand-acre park, just inside the fence, and Alan had recommended my following it and keeping an eye on the fence for signs of damage, so that it could be repaired before the deer found their way out and onto the paved road. We watched for the elk, too, especially the aging bull somewhere in the woods known for his cantankerous and aggressive behavior. Peter told me stories about him as we drove. There was a body of elk legend in the Deer Park that went back through generations of elks and humans. Alan would tell me some of the same stories Peter had told me, with more details, and a seasoned, proprietary pleasure. As we drove, even when we were talking, the sounds and the hush of the deep woods enveloped us and dwarfed our voices. We found that we were speaking quietly, and then that we had stopped speaking and were driving slowly in silence, with the snore of the jeep as a low, hoarse continuo.

Handy kept checking on how my driving was coming along, and one afternoon when he judged I was ready he climbed in beside me—without Peter—and we drove to the gate of the Deer Park and then out onto the highway. There were few cars in those days. The cement road was empty for long stretches of time and distance, in the middle of the day, with an expectant, settled stillness, but it seemed exposed and unpredictable and frightening to me. I gripped the wheel and tried to do exactly what Handy asked me to do, driving along in top gear, shifting down, braking, looking in the rear-view mirror, signaling to cars as they appeared behind us to tell them to go by, then stopping on the shoulder, turning around, driving back and down the hill to the edge of Hackettstown, around a block, and back again. We did that for several days, with Handy quietly ignoring every manifestation of my anxiety, and finishing his lessons with some mechanical rudiments, like checking the oil and the battery water, and when not to open the radiator cap, and how to put up the canvas top and take it down. How to make the jeep mine, in a sense, when I needed it.

Handy extended the driving lessons, getting me to go around other blocks in Hackettstown, and eventually into the town itself, stopping at intersections, letting cars out of parking spaces in front of me, turning left at green lights, parking, pulling out into traffic, telling me what to do one block in advance, driving into the gas station, filling up on Alan's account, and one day taking a back road over to a small neighboring town.

Finally the day came when he thought it might be time for me to sign up for an official driving test. I parked in front of the yellow frame municipal building on the main street of Hackettstown, and as calmly as possible filled in the papers applying for a license, and then with an inspector beside me followed his instructions, backed out into the main street and drove around Hackettstown, turning at traffic lights as I had done with Handy, driving up and down steep hills, signaling, parking, turning around and driving back along the main street. And passing. Trying to act as though it were something I did all the time. Then I was shown into a back room with desks like a schoolroom and given the form for the written test. The old building had been set on a slope, so that the front of it was at ground level but the room at the back was one story up, and the open windows looked straight out into the limbs of oaks and maples, with the breeze whispering through the leaves. It seemed to me only a few weeks, surely not more than a month or so, since I had sat in that other upstairs room, in the first warm days of spring, in Pennsylvania, with the windows open among the new leaves, to take the College Entrance Examination, without even knowing, when I had the form in front of me, what college I was taking it for. This time the test seemed to be something of a formality. I was grown up now. And Handy had brought back for me from town a little manual of the New Jersey driving laws and instructions on which the test would be based. I knew the answers to the questions, and when I had completed the test I waited out in the front room, and a man in uniform issued me the official yellow card allowing me to drive on my own.

Handy and I walked to the jeep, with me trying to think of what I could give him, to thank him. I could not take him for a drink, for a start. He rejected the very mention of it, and I could only guess why, for he would not say a word about it. As we drove back and turned into the Deer Park, the question nagged me, through my muffled elation at having my new license. Handy appeared to take the license for granted and to regard his own part in my getting it as all in the day's work, like fetching the groceries. What could I give him? Nothing I could think of was right. Not clothes, or books. Fishing gear? He told me he did not fish. Not

even companionship: where could we go, what could we do together, outside the routine of his days as the caretaker at the
house? Everything I thought of seemed to allude to distances that
I had never realized were between us. When I next saw Alan and
told him about the license, I asked him what I could do for Handy
to thank him, and I saw that the question stopped him too, and
appeared to take him by surprise. He said, "Don't worry. I'll take
care of it." I said I wanted to give Handy something myself, and
asked him what it could be. He said again, "I'll take care of it." If I
managed to get Handy some small token, that summer, I am sure
he accepted it correctly and without any expression that I could
interpret, but all these years later I am convinced that I never
really managed to thank him.

15

Alan came on weekends, usually, and sometimes turned up in the middle of the week. He would be there, suddenly, to our surprise, and then it would turn out that Mary and Handy had known he was coming: he'd called them and they hadn't told us. Alan got me to drive him to the lake, with Peter in the backseat, to check on my driving, and he gave me a few tips, about shifting down before tight corners and easing my way over rocks and roots, and generally he seemed to approve, not only of my handling of the jeep but of the way Peter and I seemed to be getting along, and of what he could tell of our morning studies. I liked the math part of them no better than Peter did, but we managed our daily pages of the book, and we had a reading schedule for history and literature that went far beyond Peter's school curriculum, but dutifully included all of it. Peter loved Stevenson's *Kidnapped* and *Treasure Island,* and when he came to Swift's *Gulliver's Travels* he read—sometimes aloud— with great excitement and amusement.

On one of our early trips along the tracks through the Deer Park, Peter and I had come to the mansion. The track descended a slope in the woods, and all at once there it was, standing by itself in its clearing, a very large frame house painted brown, so that it looked like a free-standing shadow in the forest, a jagged shape with curved corners, a wide porch coiled around it, the roof sections rising several stories to the tops of round towers, elaborate gray-green lightning rods, filigreed combs of gray metal along the roof peaks, all one solitary looming silence, with the trees whispering around it. We got out and stood looking up at it, and went up the wide steps that cracked and echoed under our feet, leaving our footprints in the dust, waving through spiderwebs as we stepped onto the porch with its broad ornate banister curving up to friezes of dowelled ornamentation below the eaves. The porch went on echoing our feet, the sound coming from another century.

The shutters were closed outside the long windows. They too were covered with the same gray film of dust that lay like a shadow on the steps, the porch, the banisters. We tried to peer in but the curtains were drawn inside, and Peter told me what he remembered in there. This was the living room, this was the dining room. I asked whether the house was ever used now, and Peter said yes, but not really. Nobody lived there. Alan was always going to open it up and spend some time there, but it had been a long time since anyone had done that. "My grandfather lived here sometimes," he said. "I think it was my great-grandfather who built it. He was the one who brought the elks, I think."

"Did you ever see the house when it was open?"

"Oh yes," Peter said. "I remember people here in the dining room, in the middle of the day, and seeing it all lit up, with lights hanging in the trees all around it."

"When was that?"

"I don't know. I was small. Just—very small." Then, after a minute he said, "But this is where I'm going to live someday." He said it again, when we got back into the jeep.

Then when Alan came and the three of us drove down to the lake, Peter asked whether we could go to the mansion and see inside. Alan said he had been meaning to do that, and we made our way through the woods to the slope where the house suddenly emerged below us, and I realized as it appeared that it had seemed to me to be a ghost, and that I was surprised to see it standing there again.

16

I had loved empty, uninhabited houses ever since I was a child. I suppose most children do. An empty house was a found dream, part of it forgotten, but perhaps not beyond recall. I had even seen two ghost houses, one when I was younger than Peter, and the other a few years later.

I had come to the first of them on one of the unplanned and unexpected outings with my father that occurred seldom in my childhood and were never repeated, so that each was startling and unique.

The day I remembered was during the years in Scranton, when the wasteland between us was at its most desolate. In later years, when I came to think of it, one of the odd things about my father's demeanor toward me during that time was how completely it was confined to my childhood. Once I had reached college years, after he came back from the army, he was distant, but helplessly so, without hostility, like someone adrift in himself without oars. But when I was a child, his behavior toward me, with its fixed, watchful, tight severity, was in sharp contrast to his indulgent kindly manner with other children of my own age, in Sunday school, for example. Whatever it may have been in either of us that kept him from simple affections toward me at that time, he did not normally give any thought to my company, and occasionally spoke of being much too busy for that. When he did take me along somewhere—on a round of house calls, for instance, during which I waited in the car while he visited each house—he remained preoccupied and moody, off in his own projects and considerations, and likely to be impatient if addressed. But from time to time some twinge of guilt, intimation of inadequacy, sentimental resolution, or random loneliness suggested to him that we should *do* something, and have some real time, as he said, together. When he spoke of it that way it made me feel hot in the face, and uncomfortable, and when the real time together started he seemed to have forgotten it, and to have returned to his distant and unapproachable self.

On a day in spring when the weather seemed to have really turned, and the sky was clear, the air sunlit and balmy, the green buds just beginning to appear on the bare branches, he decided that he and I should go for a drive up the West Mountain and have a picnic together. He loaded a few things to eat into the trunk of the car and we drove up the mountain, starting on dirt roads that I took when I hiked there. It was strange, driving over them in a car, and with him, as though something needed to be explained. I thought that, as usual, he had other things in mind besides this outing of ours—some member of the congregation whom he wanted to visit for some reason, or maybe some piece of property that somebody wanted to sell. I could not tell whether he knew where he was going. We drove off the road I knew onto one where I had never been, and followed it for some miles along the slope until it was no more than a farm track, a pair of tractor ruts with a grassy ridge between them. He edged off the road into an overgrown pasture behind the remains of a wall, parked, and unpacked the food he had brought.

He acted as though he knew the place, but I had no idea when or in what circumstances he might have come there before. A few rocks had been arranged in a horseshoe shape for an open fireplace, and he set about trying to light a fire there. He did not ask for my help, or seem to want any. He was not paying any attention to me at all. Maybe he was thinking. Maybe he had forgotten that I was there. The fallen sticks and branches lying around were damp with the spring rains. He crumpled newspaper and hot dog cartons and piled kindling on them and lit the paper in several places, but the fire would not catch. He bent down and took the sticks off and got more paper to repeat the process. He took off his hat and jacket and bent over in his white shirt and pulled the twigs into a pile on the paper, and blew on the paper when the flame was shrinking away. He looked awkward and undignified, and I could feel that he would not be pleased to be seen that way, failing to get the fire lit, wadding and lighting more paper as I watched. Finally I asked whether it would be all right for me to walk down the lane a little way and see what was there. He said yes, but not to go far, and to come right back.

I walked along the ruts, the mud holes, the tufts of hueless late winter grass with new green coming through at the roots. The track looked as though no one had passed that way for a long time. Not since before the winter, maybe. There were thin branches lying across it where they had fallen. I could see overgrown pasture land beyond the wall to my left, woods on the other side, and then the track went straight ahead but was grassed over as though no longer used, and the ruts turned sharply to the right between two other half tumbled walls. I followed the ruts, and where they bent to the left, a hundred yards or so from the turnoff, I came to an old disused barn on the right, its wide, dark, unpainted boards cupped and cracked, showing night and day between them, its roof sagging, and gone here and there, its big doors awry and the dead grass grown high and pale against them. Just past the barn there was an opening in the wall on the left, through which the ruts led in to a clearing in front of a house. A plain, two-story building, with brick chimneys at either end. It was painted light gray, with white trim around the doors and windows and on the uprights of the banisters. It looked as though the paint was new, put on not longer ago than the summer before. The windows were clean, too, as though they had been washed very recently, and I could see through the front panes clear across the house and out through the back. The rooms looked completely empty. There was no sign of fresh vehicle tracks or of trodden grass around the front steps. Behind the house there was another barn, painted, and in better repair than the first one. I stood examining the silent place, wanting to explore it and find out about it but hesitant about approaching the front door, feeling that I had been gone long enough, and I turned and went back.

My father had got the fire going and unwrapped the hotdogs and buns. He asked where I had been for so long and was pleased with his fire and this impromptu escapade, and was not annoyed. We stood avoiding the smoke, eating our hot dogs. He had brought some buttermilk to drink out of the bottle.

I asked him whether he knew anything about the empty farmhouse up the road to the right.

"What farmhouse?" he asked.

"Just a little way up there and around to the right. It looks as though nobody's living in it, but it's well taken care of. It's got new paint on it."

"There isn't any farmhouse up that way."

"I saw it. I could look right through the windows."

"Don't tell stories. There isn't any farmhouse up there."

"But I saw it."

"Don't tell stories." The word, for my parents, was a way of not saying "lies."

I said nothing for a minute, and we chewed. Then I said, "Will you walk up there with me and look, when we've finished eating?"

Somewhat to my surprise he agreed to do that, and when we had packed the remains of the picnic into the back of the car we walked up the track and turned right and went on to the bend, but there was no barn on the right, and beyond there, to the left, there was no building of any kind. I said I didn't understand it, and my father said he did not want to hear another word about it.

There was a boy in school who had been born in a house far up on the mountain, and whose older brothers still lived there as year-round hunters. I did not know him very well, but I asked him about the place, describing the way to get to it as well as I could, though I was not sure that he understood where I meant. He shook his head. Then he said, "Maybe I know where you mean. I think there used to be a house up around there somewhere. I think it was sold for the wood and things. Maybe my brother bought some of it."

Then two or three years later my father actually did buy an old farmhouse. I cannot imagine where the money came from. I think he said the place went for $1,500. His salary was $3,600 and the church was in arrears with that. Someone must have arranged things for him. The small house stood beside a dirt road, west of Hazleton, in the center of Pennsylvania, beyond several prosperous, well-kept Amish farms. It was a plain dwelling behind two big trees, with the two front windows facing the road, a narrow porch one step up from the ground, two tiny bedrooms upstairs, a kitchen, and then a further outdoor kitchen behind it. My mother frowned on the whole enterprise, or what she knew about it, no doubt for sound practical reasons, but by that point in their marriage she was likely to frown on any venture that he got up to, off on his own, with the car, which she could not drive. He took her there, and showed her the chicken-wired plot out in front where the last tenant still tended a vegetable garden, with cucumber vines trailing among the tomato plants and young cabbages, and my father talked to the tenant about the village of Rimerton, on the Allegheny, where he had been born, and my mother shook her head, and clucked her tongue at the kitchen.

My father had been driving down to that part of the state, doing work for the Juvenile Court in Scranton, visiting a reform school near State College, and had found the place through friends he had met, "congenial folks" living down the road, the man a teacher at the college and his wife a great reader. My mother and she became friends, but even so my mother did not go down to the house very often. My father rustled up a few volunteers from the congregation to go with him to help renovate the late nineteenth-century house, paint it, wallpaper it, clean it out. He got a free load of lime from the State, somehow, since the place was officially a farm, with a small barn out in back, and a well and pump house, and quite a few acres of fields, which my father rented out to a neighbor. I shared his excitement about houses in general and this one in particular, and went with him a few times on weekends.

The white pyramid of lime settled in between the kitchen door and the red barn, a proof of something, and my father had a row of willow posts planted along the lane that led between his fields down to the valley in back. They began to sprout in the spring as they were meant to, turning into a row of young willow trees. I was older by then. I was no longer intimidated by him. He said, on those trips, that we were "off on our own," suggesting a conspiracy against the women of the family. He did not walk anywhere, and when I wanted to explore I simply told him that I was going.

The ground was layered with outcrops of shale and was said to be full of rattlesnakes, though I never saw any. A neighbor's pigs were allowed to run loose in the fields below the house, supposedly to keep the snakes down. I walked along the lane to the bottom of the fields and on into the woods, still on the land my father had bought. I did not know whether he had ever walked the bounds of it himself. The lane must have been used only by the farmer next door, who rented the fields and cut firewood in the woods. It led down to the creek, flowing there under low trees, which was my father's boundary.

Across the creek, downstream, among big trees, I saw a small cabin painted yellow. A dog chain trailed from the porch near the front door. Whoever lived there, I thought, must be out with the dog, and I walked on up through the woods some distance until the tracks ended in a field of buckwheat. I went on through the woods but found no path, and turned back.

The dog chain was still running out to no dog as I passed the yellow cabin, and I saw no signs of anyone there, and went on back to the house. I told my father that I had walked back to the creek at the end of his land. He said nothing to indicate whether he had actually ever been there himself.

"Whose land is it on the other side?"

"Farmer over that way," he said, pointing vaguely along the dirt road.

"Is that his little cabin, by the creek?"

"There's no cabin over there."

"I just saw it. There's a dog chain by the front door. Somebody's living there."

"There wasn't any cabin down there."

"Have you been down there?"

"The first time I came. I didn't see any house."

"Maybe they just built it. But it looks as though it's been there a while."

Then he seemed to forget about it. The next day I walked down to the creek again and there was no cabin on the other side.

The neighbor who taught at the state college had lived there for several years, and was interested in the history of the area. One day I asked him whether there had ever been a cabin down on the other side of the creek. He said, "I think there used to be some kind of building down there. It fell down a long time ago." That seemed to be all he knew, and I said nothing about it to my father.

17

When I saw them, nothing about those houses had suggested to me that they were apparitions, some kind of waking dream. But the mansion at the Deer Park was ghostly even when we walked on the solid floor of the porch and tried to get our fingers around the edges of the shutters to peer through at the muffled panes. It remained like something seen through water or some less familiar element, even when Alan stood at the foot of the steps and looked around him at the dogwoods and sumacs under the beeches and oaks, the low branches that had moved closer to the house than he remembered them, and now were used to having the place to themselves. Whoever looked after the house when he was not there, whether it was Harold or one of the tenant farmers who came through the other gate on the far side of the Deer Park, had kept an area around the house cleared, and the mowed grass looked pale, so that the house appeared to be standing in its spellbound circle, at the foot of a sunbeam, in the middle of the forest. Alan walked up the loud steps, took out his key, raised it to the lock, and then turned and held it out to Peter.

"You let us in," he said.

Peter opened the door slowly into the sleep of the place, the deep smell of dust and dustcovers and old wood and mildew, all sunk in shadow, with the curtains drawn, the shutters locked, the walls enclosing a hush that was not quite silence but a kind of gray monotone. From some far-off room in the place a note, like a faint chime, a glass bowl or metal object touched once, came to us, and we stood listening.

"Chipmunks," Alan said. In front of us a flight of broad stairs with a cataract of carpet in the middle, and an unfurled banister, rose into the dusk. I was startled to find a figure standing beside me, close enough to touch me, motionless, not alive. As my eyes got used to the dimness I saw that it was a standing suit of armor.

Alan disappeared around a corner and drew back curtains, raised blinds, let in more light, and then opened windows and the shutters outside them, and the day found us. Everywhere there were mammoth shapes in dustcovers. Following old habits, Alan moved from window to window letting the light and air in, and then going on to other rooms while Peter and I explored more slowly. Most of the house, as it was then, must have been built in the years following the Civil War, the heyday of the robber barons, some of whom had been friends of Alan's grandfather. That had been the age of the self-righteous terminations known as the plains wars. Through the seizure of the West with its massacres and justifying, the floors and turrets and Tiffany windows had gone up here, under the hands of carpenters from Allamuchy and Tranquility and Hackettstown whose experience included building and repairing churches where they sang in the choirs and thought of being saved, and hotels in whose bars they gathered on Saturdays. They brought in wagonloads of beams and raised them in the clearing, and somewhere in one of the rooms, in a desk to which Alan carried the key, there was probably still a yellowed printed program of the ceremonial opening, with a guest list of politicians and bankers from New York, and the governor of the state and local clergy, and maybe an Episcopal bishop, a menu, the program of the small concert. There had been other buildings at that time, out under the trees. An outdoor kitchen for the summertime, carriage houses and a stable, and garden structures. There had been a small formal rose garden with a statue, decently draped, one arm raised, in the middle of the far hedge, against the woods. There had been a croquet lawn, and rockers on the porch surveying it all, and cigar smoke and gossip and talk of money and politics and the financing of railroads and Custer and Bismarck, Fisk, Gould, and the scandals of Erie. Reminiscences of the canals. The Johnstown Flood. Fishing and hunting. All cooked for and waited on in virtual silence by colored servants from South Carolina, some of whom remembered slavery.

We were turning slowly and walking through the dust of it, over its carpets, lifting dustcovers to reveal empty elephant's feet, touching the reflections on its closed piano, pausing before the long window of its tall clock with the pendulum holding the faces of sun and moon hanging motionless, waiting for the return of time.

We wandered through the rooms, losing sight of each other, noticing that we were alone. Alan had gone up another flight of stairs somewhere, opening windows in the upper stories. He said he wanted to air the place out. Both he and Peter needed to visit it. I went slowly through rooms, examining, touching—a tiger's teeth, which seemed real, the edge of a tapestry—staring up at paintings that might have been by Inness or Whittredge or Bierstadt, or imitators of theirs. Then Alan reappeared and was telling me about the place, what he remembered there, how Peter loved it. He wanted to show me the kitchen. He opened closets and peered around inside. Mothballs. Croquet mallets and a table umbrella and folding chairs.

"I'm going to open this up again," Alan said. "Maybe next month. We used to do that in the summer. Open it up and stay here for a while. Great parties. Went on for days. One time after a Princeton reunion we came on up here. We had more help in those days. But we can still get some more in if we need to. Peter would like to stay over here."

"Has he ever done that?"

"When he was very small. Louis liked to have it open in the summer and stay here, and I stayed over at the Deer Park house. They came in through the other gate, toward Tranquility. That's only a few years ago. My God, I can't believe it."

He led me into the kitchen, checked closets and fire extinguishers. "It could burn to the ground before anybody knew a thing about it," he said, and opened a fuse box, threw a switch, threw it off again. The huge kitchen was full of hulking dark forms. Vast tables in the middle, great black stoves, sinks near the back door, a refrigerator like a bank vault, cupboards loaded with stacked kitchen equipment waiting like the pendulum. I noticed, with a certain surprise, that the kitchen smelled like the kitchen in the basement of my father's church in Scranton.

"We managed," Alan said. "Louis was the last one really to use it. My father spent the summers here when they weren't in Europe. Before that, my grandfather had it open all summer, and they used to come up here for a week or two at Thanksgiving and Christmas. New Year's up here. And people wanted to come out and see the elk. My grandfather had stories about the elk he liked to tell when he had a chance to. He was in the living room one day with some friends when some photographer who had an appointment to see him came by. Horse and buggy from somewhere. He wanted to take pictures of the elk for a Sunday rotogravure section of the *Times*. My grandfather probably reeled off a few of his elk stories, and he liked to tell how he said to the man, 'You can bring your cameras and all that and I'll see that they let you in, but

I have these witnesses that I'm telling you now it's at your own risk entirely. I can't be responsible for the bull elk's disposition. You may never see him at all, but if you do, and he goes for you, don't come to me about it—if you can still go to anybody.' And the fellow agreed, and came back with a buckboard and tripods and a load of glass plates and went out and shouted until the elk came, and he got a few pictures. But apparently he outstayed his welcome, from the bull's point of view, or he tried to get too close or something. And when he was down under his black hood trying to get the elk in focus, upside-down, the big head and the antlers came down and the bull charged him. The poor guy took off for the back of the wagon and jumped on with the elk right after him, and when he jumped into the wagon the bull jumped in after him, and he got bashed around and hurt before he managed to crawl into the driver's seat and pick up the reins and get out of there. He never sued. There are some old photographs of the elk even from those days. I don't know who took them. There were a lot more elk in those days. There's only that one old bull now and he's pretty lazy, but if you call for him you want to have a tree nearby. Sometimes he won't get out of the road. And don't get out of the jeep if he does that. He smashed somebody's headlight and radiator a few years ago because they were a little too impatient to get past him."

Alan went on up the back stairs from the kitchen and I followed, and Peter found us, and we walked through the big bedrooms, with the canopied beds tented with dustcovers, but the windows open onto the bright grass of the clearing below.

"Just close the windows," Alan said. "I'll tell them we've been over, and get them to come back and give it a good airing, until we can open it up."

18

Beyond the far gate of the park the lane led down through the woods to a paved country road and several small houses that were part of Alan's estate. He took me along to meet friends of his who were staying in one of them, an English couple with a little boy, in the States for a short time on some kind of import-export business. The man was attached to a firm in India. He was taking a new Packard convertible back with him to sell there—he already had the buyer—driving it himself in the meantime. All three of them seemed perpetually and impossibly clean and well turned out, and in whatever circumstances slightly overdressed, like mannequins in advertisements, and they were infallibly polite, agreeable, and distant. They came to the lake in the Deer Park for a swim a few times, praying for the Packard on the park roads, and Alan added to the distance between us by warning Peter and me in an undertone not to crowd them, but to let them have their privacy. From the cabin steps Peter and I watched them take out the canoe, as though they were borrowing it from us for some unavoidable but risky venture. The atmosphere around them emanated from the primness of the young woman, and her treatment of the child—who indeed appeared to be a kind of miniature —as though he might easily break. As far as we knew he had no one to play with.

Once when Alan could not get out to the Deer Park for some reason and wanted Peter and me to join him in New York, the man drove us to town in the Packard, talking to us more freely than usual, about India and the circles he moved in there. He said he had done this before, on an earlier trip: buying a new Packard in the States and taking it back with him when he went, to sell for a price that sounded like a fortune, to some nabob. The last time, he said, the sling on the crane had broken when they were unloading the car in India at the dock, and the car had fallen upside-down, flattening the whole top of it, but they had rebuilt it out there, and the accident had not seriously reduced the price that had been agreed on.

In another of the houses on the estate Alan introduced me to an immaculately dressed old man, a brother or cousin of his mother, the late Belgian Princesse de Caraman-Chimay. He was very thin, elegant, and fragile-looking. I never saw him dressed otherwise than in a light gray three-piece suit in that small house in the country. He gave no indication that he either spoke or understood—or wished to entertain—any language except French, and once he had shaken my hand without looking at me, he paid no more attention to me than if I had not been there. After Alan explained to him what I was doing at the Deer Park and laboriously involved me in a few exchanges with this personage, he referred later to my stiff phrases in those circumstances as evidence of my hopelessly bookish and archaic French. Alan's harshness in that case, I think, reflected some discomfort of his own in the company of this dried kinsman of his, who seemed to be a model of discontent. Alan had brought him a case of wine, because there was nothing locally available that was fit for him to drink. I helped Alan unload other boxes of delicacies for the house, and the two of them talked about food, about the minor virtues and the unfailing inadequacies of the cook whom Alan had arranged to take care of him, and about family news—another Belgian princess coming for a visit, as the Queen of Belgium had done a few years earlier—until the loose old fingers brushed mine in token of parting.

There were still a dozen or more tenant farms in a deep crescent around that side of the Deer Park, an arrangement that apparently had been set up before the Dutch colony was taken over by the English in the seventeenth century, and had survived the Revolution and wars and social changes that came after it— three hundred years during which the region had escaped most of the changes that happened around it. The main line from New England to Philadelphia and Washington was some distance to the east, and the route from central Pennsylvania to New York City lay to the south, and so the Deer Park enclave had retained some ways and assumptions and appearances of a past that had been all but forgotten on all sides of it. Alan took me to meet a few of the farming families, and spoke to me a little about the ancient arrangement. It sounded like an ordinary landlord-tenant relationship, with long-term assumptions—in most cases going back for generations—on both sides. Alan had known the families we stopped to see all his life, and they knew a fair amount about him and his family, and surely believed rumors beyond that. But as we drove away from those visits, it was plain that Alan did not foresee the setup lasting much longer. Too many things were pulling it apart. The days of the family farm, in any circumstances, were numbered. Children moved away. Taxes and urban sprawl favored turning land into real estate. I could hear in Alan's voice his own gradual withdrawal as part of the overall fraying.

He took me to Tranquility to see the old country church, with the long sheds for horses and buggies on rainy or snowy Sundays. A pretty, nineteenth-century white frame building with a spire, in the colonial style. One weekend when Dorothy was at the Deer Park, Alan, to my surprise, suggested that we might go to the morning service, and I agreed. It sounded as though we would all be going together, but at the last minute it turned out that Alan was not going, and neither was Peter. But Alan urged it upon us. It was something we should see, and my reluctance ceded to Alan's persistence and to my own curiosity. I could remember country churches in western Pennsylvania where I had gone as a child, in tow to my father, in my white buck wing-tip shoes that looked much too big for me, to be watched out of the corners of eyes from behind raised hymn books. To be uncomfortable and welcomed and made still more uncomfortable, and Tranquility was a kindly echo of those churches, in a different accent, and whatever curiosity we had brought was turned back on us until at last we escaped to the woods of the Deer Park.

19

Some afternoons I drove in the jeep by myself along the shaded tracks through the woods, drifting along with the top down. I saw the elk several times, always when I was alone. There were two or three elk does, and many deer in the woods. The summer days were hot. The deer and the elk stopped grazing, looked up in surprise, bolted or stood and watched me as I passed. Once when the bull had looked up toward me I slowed to a stop and sat watching him, with my foot on the accelerator. When he began to walk slowly toward me I moved on, and he stood still and went on looking.

Once as I came over a rise under the big limbs and coasted down the other side I felt a swift cool rush of air on my head and down the back of my neck, and an instant later I saw a dark six- or seven-foot wingspan glide down in front of the jeep and sail ahead of me like a torn shred of night. It was the golden eagle. If I had reached up as it went over me I could probably have touched it.

Occasionally, if I thought about it, I had a rifle in the jeep. Alan and Harold had suggested it, complaining about groundhogs, and cattle breaking their legs in groundhog holes. But that was on the farms. There were no cattle in the park. I took the rifle along with a certain embarrassment, as though I were wearing a bit of costume in town. As a child I had been forbidden not only to own a toy gun of any kind but ever to point my finger as though it were a gun. Around the age of ten I saved up my dime a week allowance and bought a fifty-cent cap pistol, which could stand comparison with those of the other boys in the back alley. I cherished the smell of it, of the burnt cap paper and the metal barrel and imitation pearl handle. My mother knew about the gun, but it was kept from my father as a deadly secret, during one of the worst periods of my parents' soured marriage and of my watchful relation to him. One day as he returned from conducting a funeral, stepping in his cutaway from the door of the funeral director's Pierce Arrow, he saw me with the cap pistol, playing with the other boys in the alley (which was also forbidden), and a terrible scene followed that involved my mother as well as me.

In my last year in college, as a gesture of liberation from such prohibitions, I took some money I had earned and bought a target rifle in a sporting goods store on Nassau Street. Then a young member of the English faculty and I went, for several afternoons, to a ravine in the woods outside town where other people went to shoot at tin cans, and we fired away at cans while talking about Dostoevsky and Mann.

The rifle was dangerous in the jeep, and really had no purpose. It rode around behind the seat, and I did not shoot anything. But a neighboring farm boy and I went out twice, walking in the pastures outside the park, looking for groundhogs. Alan, when he heard about it, laughed and said from then on that I would shoot anything that moved, and I wondered what part his own safari days, with their expensive codes, may have been playing when he said it. The first of those afternoons we simply walked and never shot at all, but the next time, with the afternoon sun dazzling on the pasture, we came over a rise and I caught sight of a groundhog standing up, and I raised the rifle as he started to run for his hole, and fired. It was unlikely that I could have hit him at that distance, but it was what is called a "lucky" shot, and he was killed instantly. When we got to him he was lying on his back, one paw in the air. I looked down and was disgusted at what I had done. I thought, "This is what is supposed to be so exciting. This creature was full of his life a minute ago, and this is what I have managed to make of him. There he is. Dead. Something I know nothing about."

"Just leave him there," the boy said. "The crows will take care of him." I stood looking down at the body already receding in death, and wanted to ask its pardon, and felt ridiculous about that and its uselessness, and the shame burned into me. There was nothing to say about it. The rifle went into a closet.

20

My driving seemed fairly reliable, although the traffic on the main roads and around the newly installed traffic circles near Heightstown still tightened my knuckles and accelerated my pulse. On Friday afternoon or Saturday morning I would check with Handy about whether he needed the jeep, and if it was free I would drive down to Princeton, to the Harrison Street housing project, and fetch Dorothy. Occasionally friends came up from Princeton on the weekends for picnics and to go swimming in the lake. Alan encouraged it, though I could guess when he was spotting telltale signs of their being "intellectuals." Bill Arrowsmith and his wife Jean came more than once, and we rigged hammocks under the trees and talked through the afternoon, with Peter in and out of the conversations. He returned to Sherlock Holmes and Marco Polo, and we to Henry James, Yeats, and Joyce and Mann.

Alain Prévost came only once, turning up one day when Alan was giving a party for young friends that began at the lake and went on into the evening at a farmhouse outside the park gate. Alain seemed distracted and overcharged that summer. I believe (my guess based partly on a novel that he later published) that he was having an affair with a woman some years older than he was, another friend of Alan's, with a big house on Long Island and a circle of rich friends—it sounded like a reincarnation of the Gatsby era—and when I was in Princeton I had no idea how to reach him.

Sometimes Alan brought friends of Peter's for a swim on weekends. During the week Peter and I went to Allamuchy almost every day to collect the mail at the general store, and into Hackettstown occasionally to check the fishing tackle, and we took to calling in often at a big brick colonial-style house above the highway, facing out over the woods of the Deer Park, where Peter's Rutherford cousins, twin boys of his own age, came for the summer. Occasionally we took them along with us into Allamuchy to the post office, and I shudder still when I remember how they loved the jeep and begged me to drive faster, as they sat in the back with the top down, and how fast I did drive, more than once, with all four of us shouting and laughing, along the concrete highway. Fortunately there was almost no traffic along that road then, but the jeep's short wheel base and high center of gravity made it precarious as the speedometer needle climbed. The prayers in my gut brought on prudence before our luck, or whatever guardian was along, gave up on us.

A few times, late in the summer, Alan drove us to New York, to his big top-floor apartment on Fifth Avenue, furnished grandly in some other life, probably by his mother, the décor part nineteenth-century European, part twentieth-century New York City lavish. Huge grand piano, fringed shawls on tables, Louis XV chairs, silver-framed photographs, including one of General De Gaulle with an inscription to Alan's mother. I am not sure now whether we were brought along to keep Peter company or to acquaint us with another aspect of Alan's life. He chatted confidentially about the politics of the building, its snobbish exclusivity, its antisemitism, which he spoke of with disapproval. But it was on one of those trips that he referred to the time in the thirties when his brother, Louis, and he had planned to join in the Spanish Civil War, on Franco's side. They may even have gone to Spain, though I believe they never saw action. My startled questions were inept, and Alan ignored them and turned the talk to other things.

I had grown up in the atmosphere of my father's unquestioned and determined Republican faith, which he relayed as though he had it from Mount Sinai. I had begun to grow away from that creed as soon as I began to think about it, in my student years. I simply woke up to discover that his notions were not mine. But even he had inconsistencies that he must have been carrying from somewhere in his own youth. He could not hear the name Carnegie (as in Lake Carnegie at Princeton, or the various libraries and museums) without saying, "If he had paid his workers a decent wage he might not have had so much money to give away in his own memory." It was a sentiment that he had almost certainly picked up on the streets of Pittsburgh, from people who remembered the Homestead Steel Strike and the Pinkertons, but it was evident that he liked its trenchant ring. He claimed proudly that his mother had allowed John L. Lewis to hold in her cellar some of his early, secret—indeed, "underground"—meetings of what would become the United Mine Workers. He had no details of that, when I got around to asking, and I have never been sure whether it was true. But although at least one of his sisters, a narrow, hardheaded, mean-spirited woman, was a vehement racist, my father was always openly and firmly opposed to racial discrimination of any kind.

During my childhood his political stance, however he had come to it, reached me less obviously than the prohibitions that came from his own upbringing and temperament, and from his religious fundamentalism, which I encountered again at the Seminary when he was away in the army. That seemed to me an extension of something in my father that I had outgrown and would no longer tolerate. But politics, during my first years in college, was like watching a card game I did not really understand, played by people I did not know. It was the year I went to the Deer Park, and I listened to friends, including the revered Richard Blackmur and Bill Arrowsmith, speaking with passion about the coming election, expressing their dread at the thought of Thomas Dewey being elected to the presidency, which seemed likely, and other friends talking urgently of their hopes for Henry Wallace. That spring and summer the political arena, and what was involved in it, began to seem real to me. My own readings in history began to take their place in that. Arrowsmith would be talking about the poetry of Wallace Stevens one minute and Rousseau's Social Contract, and its relevance to us, the next. I began to recognize my own sympathies and convictions, and see that they were liberal, however unformed and unfocused they might be. And when I learned of Alan's and Louis's adherence to Franco, and some of Alan's other political assumptions, they seemed to me not only startling and repellent but discredited, done for, like bits of wallpaper in a demolition site, or obiter dicta of the Red Queen.

On one of those trips to New York Alan stopped in the suburbs to pick up a school friend of Peter's, a red-haired shy boy named Andrew, and he took Andrew and his father along with us to the city. Later, Alan told me that he had decided to go to France the following summer, to the villa on the Côte d'Azur, on St. Jean Cap-Ferrat, which he had inherited from his mother. He asked whether I—Dorothy and I—would be interested in coming along to look after Peter and Andrew, whom he had invited to come to keep Peter company. The question took me by surprise, but it was easy to answer, and we began at once to imagine France, the Riviera. Peter was as excited by the idea as we were, and talked about the villa with a wild incoherence that utterly failed to convey an image of it, even after he had found a photograph album and shown us some old pictures of the place.

All through the rest of that summer at the Deer Park we talked of France, next year. Peter wondered whether he had forgotten his French, and was bashful about speaking it to Alan. One of the last weekends there, friends of Alan's whom I had not met before came to the Deer Park for the day. One of them was Maria Antonia da Braganza, an attractive woman several years younger than Alan, who was the sister of Don Duarte da Braganza, the pretender to the Portuguese throne. She had been married to a cousin of Alan's by the name of Chanler, and Alan and she talked of her beloved house up the Hudson in Duchess County. Among Alan's other guests that day there were several women whose talk with me turned to books, which surprised me in Alan's house. A couple of them actually asked me what I hoped to write, and I was so startled that I found myself answering at far too great a length, and rather pompously. It did not seem to bother Maria Antonia— or perhaps she did not hear it. She said nothing about books at all, but she and I seemed to get along at once, and after lunch she asked me to take a walk with her.

We walked out to a bank of rocks that was the ruin of some old building and sat down. She took out a case of slender cigars, offered me one, and took one herself. When they were lit she told me, in her husky voice and slight, charming accent, that Alan and she had been talking about me. I had no idea what that might mean. She said that the Portuguese government had agreed to allow the royal family to return to Portugal, more or less without conditions, and that she had been offered a house there for the coming winter and was hoping to go back. She had two boys by her former husband, Alan's cousin. The children had joint American and Portuguese citizenship, and she did not want them to lose their English if they went back to Portugal. She wondered whether I would like to join her and tutor the boys in English, after our next summer in France. We would have our own house, she said, and all our meals and living expenses. The salary itself would not be much—one *conto* a month, which came to around forty dollars—but we would be living in the country, with nothing to spend it on, and if we needed more we could talk about it later. I could not see that there was more than one possible answer, but there was Dorothy's job. To her it seemed a small thing in comparison with the chance to go to Portugal in such circumstances.

At the end of the summer, on the last day at the Deer Park house, Alan sat with Dorothy and me in the living room and said that as a way of thanking me for the summer he wanted me to choose some object from the house, anything I wanted. It was a regal offer. There were valuable things in every room. I chose a pair of square Mexican jadeite candlesticks that I had admired all summer. I knew they were modern, not museum pieces, and it seemed all right to choose those. I have managed to hang on to them, through a series of moves, all these years.

21

That winter of 1948–1949 we tried to imagine France, and Portugal
—which was even harder—and Europe. They remained somewhere between history and the world we knew, invisible despite
whatever we had read. I remembered as a small child asking my
mother great, persistent questions, among them, "Mother, what
is Europe? *Where* is Europe?"

The *Nyhorn* was scheduled to take over a week on its voyage to
Genoa, and during that time, in the summer weather, it acquired
the familiarity and the comfortable tedium of a temporary home.
In one of the games with Peter and Andrew I slipped on the wet
iron deck plates, under an iron companionway ladder, and laid my
shin bare, so that I limped around for a few days (later I thought of
that companionway as a prophetic signal), and we sat in the sun,
more than was good for us, and read. We got to know where the
mice lived on board, and their routes along the bulkheads, their
daytime scheduled runs. One of the other passengers, a thin,
laconic young man from Arkansas who had been a bombardier in
Europe, told us about finding mice in the bomber, barely conscious

with the cold and the lack of oxygen. He and his crew mates decided that the mice would never make it through the flight, however they had managed to survive up until then, and so they tied the corners of handkerchiefs to their tails to make parachutes and dropped them through the bomb bay doors, watching the slipstream snatch the handkerchiefs, and imagining them drifting down into the temperature of the world again. It was another story, like those of the Italian seaman, that seemed less likely the more I thought about it, but stories of that kind were a leitmotif of our days on the freighter. We listened to them, and they accompanied us, in the way that Peter's much-thumbed Conan Doyle stories, and the Prose Edda, which we both read and talked about, and my Yeats and Dante and Huizinga, contributed their colors and dimension to our passage, as did the flying fish bursting like spray ahead of the bow wave, and the trails of phosphorescence unfurling alongside us through the summer nights. We got to know the crew members a little, and learned that the prevailing bad smell emanating from one doorway near the galley came from a bin in which potatoes were rotting. From time to time galley hands in dirty aprons emerged from that doorway (the one the mice came from) with full garbage cans, which they tipped over the rail, laughing to us at the messy game.

The vessel's Norwegian ownership was detectable in the galley hands, the cook, and the menu, which included, at most meals, several kinds of preserved fish, cold pickled vegetables, and always potato salad—elements of what the steward (he of the routines) proudly and regularly informed us was *smorgasbord*. At the evening meal one week into the trip, he told us, as though he were letting us in on a secret, that we would be within sight of the coast of Europe the next morning. Peter and I were up on the bow before breakfast, looking ahead past the leaping showers of flying fish and the gleaming backs of the dolphins wheeling ahead of us.

There were no rays of sunlight yet in the overcast sky. Then as we strained our eyes we saw, on the horizon ahead, a slaty black line distinct from the gray sky and gray sea. The coast of Spain. We lay watching it, though it did not appear to draw any nearer. Finally we stood up, stiff and cold, and went down to breakfast, looking back over our shoulders, getting up to peer through the windows of the dining room. Then we climbed back up to watch through most of the morning, sitting on the bow with our legs swinging over the cutwater. Other passengers came and joined us, stayed for a while and left, but we ended up getting deck chairs and books and settling in. By mid-morning we could make out a long facade of cliffs falling from a serrated crest to the haze on the surface of the sea. The sheer curtain of land faced west, so the morning rays of the sun left it in its own shadow, but the sun lit up the sea between us, and shone on our faces, and on the white bridge up behind us, which now seemed to be part of ourselves, a house and memory we were bringing with us.

As we watched, another shape darkened in the gray cloud at the foot of the cliffs, a low silhouette moving certainly but imperceptibly like a shadow on a dial. A vessel. A warship, with a warship's lethal elegance. The outline, as I kept my eyes on it, was familiar, to my surprise, though at first I could not place it. Low in the water. A battleship. I did know it, I came to realize, because ten years before that I had built a model of it, and painted it a much lighter shade of gray. It was the *Missouri,* and the recognition, which could not be shared at all, was at once exciting and oddly troubling, an unexpected reminder that wherever I went I might count on some revenant from my childhood to be there ahead of me.

Closer in, after the battleship had disappeared up the coast toward the Cape Trafalgar, we saw a small town at the foot of the cliffs, and a road behind it descending from the top of the ridge. I fixed it so firmly in my eye as we approached that a year later, when I was on a bus to Algeciras and to Yeats's "heron-billed pale cattle birds," I would recognize the road I was on, and the town into which it was descending—which by then I knew was a fishing port named Tarifa—and feel that I had completed a kind of destined but unidentified circuit.

The whole morning passed in an expectant silence that the vessel seemed to know all about, but that was new to us. We slipped by the cliffs, and came in sight of others far to the right, a lower line, with more yellow in the gray, and we slid between the two and

> *came to the narrows*
> *where Hercules set up his warning markers*
> *for men, to tell them they should sail no farther . . .*

as Dante had written of the Pillars of Hercules. We had entered the Strait of Gibraltar, which he had never seen. That passage of the *Inferno*, when I had first read the poem, had gripped me more fiercely than anything I had read in the *Commedia* before, and it had remained in my head from then on, though my pronunciation must have been far from the sound of the words as Dante had known them. He was writing of Ulysses, his own image and fiction of Ulysses rather than Homer's. As far as anyone knows he never read Homer at all, but knew about him and about his Ulysses only at second hand, from Latin writers. His Ulysses was later, in every sense. Later than Homer, of course, but later than the homecoming to Ithaca, the point at which Homer ended the story in the *Odyssey*. Dante was seeing it from much later in another sense also, from an age after Paul the sailmaker and his resurrectionist legend and missionary voyages had transformed the Mediterranean world. Dante shows us his Ulysses on his last voyage out through the Pillars of Hercules into what Dante conceived of as the forbidden sea where Ulysses becomes the first (imagined) human to behold, on the other side of the earth, Mount Purgatory. The imaginary protagonist of Dante's poem would be the second. His Ulysses' late speech of exhortation to his remnant of imaginary followers was what had gripped my own mind when I was setting out, at eighteen.

> *I and my companions were old and near*
> *the end . . .*

he had said, and the word *tarde*, for "late" in the sense of "near the end," was one of the words that first caught and held me, more than seven centuries after he had written it.

> *On the one hand I left Seville behind*
> *on the other I had already left Ceuta . . .*

As they passed through the straits he spoke to them:

> *"Oh brothers," I said, "who through a hundred*
> *thousand perils have arrived at the west,*
> *do not deny to the little waking*
>
> *time that remains to your senses knowing*
> *for yourselves the world on the far side*
> *of the sun, that has no people in it . . .*

Dante represented this very speech as an epitome of the forbidden enterprise, of human pride defying divine measure, of human ambition aspiring to unlimited knowledge. But he himself, in the figure of his protagonist, Dante the pilgrim through the world of the dead, felt so deeply tempted by the apparition of Ulysses' spirit drifting in an unattached flame through the heavenless void that it nearly drew him over the edge into the abyss.

The passage kept echoing in my mind as we came through the narrows where Dante had imagined Ulysses exhorting his companions to sail toward what was, indeed, our own birthplace. I— we—were returning much, much later still from that bourne that he invoked with such warning. We were coming back when the impetus of history, and whatever temptations had led Europeans to "the far side of the sun," had found another west, another tenuous hope, a different purgatory, and had caused, and been transformed by, devastations and deaths on a scale that even Dante never dreamed of. I watched the daylight on the yellow cliffs in Africa, and then Gibraltar far to the left, until we entered the Mediterranean and the shores receded again on either side.

It was late on another day that we approached the Italian coast, and Genoa, birthplace of Columbus, who had made the westward voyage that would transform both hemispheres beyond recognition. Even if we had not known it, we could see at once that we were arriving in the aftermath of a war. The blaze of the long summer afternoon was behind us, magnified near the horizon, where the glaring white sky was flushing with the first orange and red of sunset, the deepening colors reflected onto the sea around us and onto the coast and the harbor and shoreline far ahead. We moved in more and more slowly, drawing almost to a halt far out at sea, and were met by a dark, dingy pilot vessel that communicated in some way with the bridge of the *Nyhorn,* and then turned back and led us toward the shore.

We were not being towed. The small boat the color of an old truck tire guided us very slowly while the light over the harbor and in the clouds and haze and westering light behind us filled with shades of pink and deepening mauve. We began to see some of the reasons why the approach was so cautious. Outside the harbor there was a long high breakwater, a stone and cement wall, broken in places like ancient ruins, and brushed with the same colors as the port behind it. And between us and the breached wall were the masts and superstructures of other vessels that had been sunk outside the seawall and were resting on the bottom, facing in all directions. As we came nearer we could see that some of them had capsized and were lying with their dark hulls half out of the swells. By then we were all lining the rail. The Italian merchant seaman told us that some of the vessels had been hit by bombs and some had been sunk deliberately by the Germans to block the harbor during the Allies' Italian campaign. Beyond the seawall, which was painted here and there with Cinzano advertisements in huge letters, we could see the tops of other vessels sunk inside the harbor, their rusty bridges and funnels glowing in the west light. The waves lashed the gaps in the wall that was the edge of Europe.

The Italian seaman told us that there were also mines still unexploded in the harbor, and the pilot vessel was leading us past the danger points. He said all the harbors along the coast had been mined, and boats of all kinds and sizes had been lost, coming and going. It took a long time to sweep the approaches clean. It may have been true, but the regular channel markers were in place as we came in, suggesting that the main channel was back in routine use. An old tug came out to us, and both vessels guided us slowly around the breakwater and then edged with us along the inside of it, with the port revolving around us. The *Nyhorn* was inched toward a row of towering cranes, and warped to an empty wharf as the last colors drained from the aging surfaces around us. There were a few figures down on the long wharf with railroad tracks running the whole length of it. Our own voices sounded distant, as though we were just waking, and the words called up from the wharf to our crew seemed to come from far away, incomprehensible syllables echoing in the dusk.

The steward gave me a message that had come from Alan. He was on his way. We would sleep on board that night, and he would meet us in the morning. Our last dinner was served with valedictory flourishes by the steward, and then we walked back along the yellow corridors, with their sudden, disturbing stillness, to pack our trunks, hearing the stunned sounds of the moored freighter, and already feeling like strangers in our own place. After the cabin lights were out, the light outside on the wharf shone in, with bat shadows wheeling around in it, and sounds of clanking from the railroad lines, and cranes groaning and humming along their tracks. They blocked the light as they rumbled by. Then more voices, the booming echoes of hatch covers being opened, trucks outside on the wharf. I went on deck and watched the hooks swinging over the hatches in the night full of cables and circling lights and shouts ricocheting back and forth. Finally I went back down to the cabin to lie listening to Genoa, Columbus's Genoa.

22

In the morning Alan arrived not long after breakfast. There was the Jeep station wagon parked down on the wharf. He had already spoken with the harbor officials, and he came on board with a couple of them. We went through most of the arrival formalities on the table in the dining room where we had just had breakfast. Then our trunks were taken down the gangplank and packed into the car, the last arrival procedures were taken care of at an office along the wharf, and Alan drove us through the high gates at the end of it, into Italy.

It was (I remember happily) long before the days of autoroutes, overpasses, underpasses, and of much mechanized traffic. Ours was one of the few cars. Even around the wharves there were mule carts, and more of them as we made our way through back streets to the edge of town, into thoroughfares, turning at corners between small stuccoed houses with vegetable gardens fitting tightly around them, vines deep on their walls. We edged out of town, westward, to a small road along the coast, all of us chattering, excited to be there.

The road led past beaches and followed the tops of bluffs overlooking long, inviting bays: the *Riviera di Ponente.* As the day warmed, Peter wanted to stop for a swim, and Alan pulled over to a level space on the ocean side of the road, where we looked down a bank to a stretch of sand and a few clusters of people bathing or lying in the sun. We got out and started rummaging in our belongings for bathing suits.

Since his first appearance on the freighter that morning, I had sensed an aspect of Alan that I had not glimpsed before. It seemed to be a recollection of pleasure and freedom, a reassured confidence, a savored return to a world he had missed, to a kind of ease and indulgence that he may have recalled, or imagined that he recalled, from childhood. It appeared in the way he waved aside overconcern about modesty in getting into our bathing suits, pointing out people down on the beach changing under the token screening of their towels. His manner suggested that he had returned to, and was introducing us to, a liberated Old-Worldliness that had always been part of his birthright. We changed behind the open car doors, and as Alan and the boys and I stepped naked from clothes into swimming trunks, we saw three young Italian women watching us with unabashed interest from the beach below. Alan waved, and they waved back, laughing, and it confirmed something he felt about being there. But he locked the car carefully before we left it.

After the swim in the Mediterranean we went on along the coast for a few hours, pausing at a beach with fishing boats and a restaurant for a lunch of fish and shellfish just brought in, and then at Portofino to sip mineral water and eat ices, looking down to the masts and slender decks of yachts in the protected basin below. Alan telephoned ahead to a restaurant he knew on the cliff above San Remo and made a reservation for dinner, and when we got there we were shown in to a long table beside windows open onto a wide terrace and a view of the coast and the shaded sequence of headlands below us. He had thought to order us, in advance, a risotto, gray with squid ink, and again we took our time, as Alan said we were supposed to.

The days are long in July, and after sunset the twilight seemed reluctant to darken. It was still light when we drove on toward Ventimiglia, and then the French border, the passport inspections and customs, where they waved us through. The memory of the war was still fresh, and cars were few. Americans were welcomed, and the Jeep station wagon was admired, detail by detail, as it had been wherever we stopped on the way from the wharf in Genoa.

The lights were on beyond the *corniche* and on the coast below as we made our way into France, winding around the contours of the cliffs, down to the edge of Monte Carlo and the Riviera. They were glittering around Monte Carlo, and on around the bay above Beaulieu, and were reflected in the water like banks of chandeliers. One of the major galaxies of the rich.

From Beaulieu the main road led on to Nice, but we turned sharply to the left down a narrower way that wound into St. Jean Cap-Ferrat. The café was open on the narrow *place* facing the fishing boats and moored sailboats riding the shimmering surface. We drove out onto the cape. It extends from the far side of the boat harbor like a thumb from a hand. To the right of the road an unlit, tree-shadowed hill was the Pine Wood, the *Pinède,* and to the left were the terraces and awnings of a hotel, and then a succession of large villas, one with a tower. We came to a high, pink, stuccoed wall that led to a roofed main doorway, where we stopped. Alan rang the bell, and the dark red double door swung open almost at once. They had been waiting for us. Two couples, an older pair and another a generation younger, stood on the gravel of the courtyard as we drove in, and then the men closed the doors behind us.

They welcomed Alan with a reserved, distant warmth. The tall, thin, dignified older couple expressed a weathered attachment, a commemorative affection. To him they were Joseph and Josephine, the gardener and housekeeper, who had been there since before Alan was born, but to them, as to the young man, André, and his wife, Marie-Claire, he was Monsieur. After the ceremonious greeting Alan introduced Dorothy and me, and Andrew, telling them who we were and what we were doing there. They inquired politely about the trip, and Alan opened the back of the car. Joseph produced a garden dolly, and he and André loaded our luggage onto it. Alan walked ahead of us to the steps before the terrace and the front door, talking with Josephine, and we followed, gazing around us. Somewhere not far away a dance band was playing *La Vie en Rose*.

The stuccoed walls behind us, around the garden, were the same dark raspberry pink that we had first seen along the road. It was the color of the *Villa Cucia Noya,* which rose to a tower in front of us from a wide terrace with balconies above it. Each level was edged with overhanging, dark Roman tiles. The windows and the doors were tall, relatively slender, elegant. On the far side of the villa, past the graveled paths of the garden, we could see a low wall, and beyond it the lights glittering on the bay, and beyond them the lit-up hotels of Beaulieu on the other side.

We entered a wide hall with a dark red tiled floor that ran straight through the villa onto another terrace overlooking the bay. Another suit of armor, a relative perhaps of the one in the Deer Park mansion, stood near the foot of a broad curving flight of stairs that swept upward. As we stood in the hall while Alan told André where the luggage was to be taken, we could see into the big sitting room to the left, facing the garden. The low lights in there showed tapestries on the walls. Beyond the stairs to the right, we could see the end of a dining room, along its terrace.

Alan led us out there and Josephine followed to ask whether we would like anything. She and Alan conferred and she was back in a minute with a bottle of rosé and one of seltzer, and mineral water for the boys. *La Vie en Rose* wafted up from below in waves, over and over. Alan told us that it came from a small bar and night-club that had been sneaked in on a tiny shelf of shorefront at the foot of the cliff, in a corner below the two neighboring villas on the side toward town, one of which belonged to the Singer (sewing machine) heirs, and the other to a scion of the Vanderbilts. The bar's entrepreneurs had managed to acquire a lease, no doubt by bribery, during the winter when all the owners were away, and of course the owners were outraged when they returned and found it in full swing. It was louder, Alan said, and worse for the Vanderbilt villa. It was right down beneath them, and it went on quite late. The villa's present owner had tried to get an injunction, but it had not come through yet, and now the lease was being contested in the courts, but a decision might take years, and in the meantime the pedal boats and noise were there in the daytime and the dance music went on to all hours at night. *La Vie en Rose* was the signature music of the place, recurring among tunes made familiar by Edith Piaff, and music from the twenties and thirties that Alan must have heard on wind-up Victrolas at the villa in his youth.

The terrace led along the villa to a covered arcade around the end of another, smaller, formal garden that might have been hidden in a cloister, and on the far side of that a low wall marked the top of the cliff. Beyond the wall were the sequins of light on the water, and Beaulieu. We talked quietly about the trip, in the moored daze of arrival. I was trying to imagine being where we were, and at the same time to imagine the moments, the edited, retouched, unsatisfactory glimpses that Alan was giving us, speaking with something that sounded like contentment about the villa in the scandalous but now legendary past. He alluded to his mother's drunken bouts as a fact of history, but with no details or features of the rest of her behavior, no image of what she wore or said or cared about. Nothing about his father. Nothing, either, about his brother, Peter's father, here in the villa. Alan was talking about somewhere that was his alone now, as only he remembered it.

After a while he led Peter and Andrew back in and up the stairs to their rooms in the tower. We watched his familiar flat-footed, knock-kneed tread, his American shoes with their woven tops and thick rubber soles, receding over the dark red tiles into the low light at the foot of the broad flight of stairs, and for a moment he looked homespun, awkward, someone out of our own past. We sat saying little, looking out over the bay, breathing it all, and he came down and sat with us for a moment like an old friend, and then led us up to our own room, made sure everything was there, and said good night.

He had given us a big room above the sitting room, with dark green flock wallpaper, towering mirrors, tall windows facing the bay and the far glittering shoreline. The dance music rose from below. To us who had never known the world there without it, *La Vie en Rose* and its thirties woodwinds seemed to be the sound of the place, the score that accompanied the theatrical setting and the lights across the water.

23

There was no planned order to our days, for I was no longer expected to be teaching Peter anything, though we talked, as before, about what we were reading. We passed the Norse sagas back and forth—though there was some aspect of them that Peter seemed to hold to himself like a secret, a high card—and their characters and events recurred in our conversation. Alan stayed up in his room on the telephone part of the day. Joseph was preoccupied with the garden routine, raking the paths, clearing dead leaves from the beds, trimming and pruning. He answered our questions but did not go on talking. Alan had brought a small yellow inflatable boat, military surplus, which Joseph inflated and presented to Peter and me. He showed us where he thought it should be kept: in a closed cupboard along the side of the garden toolshed. Beside the cupboard there was a stone cupola like a miniature tower, with a door in it opening to the top of a corkscrew flight of stairs. They led down through their stony smells to another door, padlocked, at the foot of the cliff. That was our way out onto the rocks of the shore, to go swimming.

And that was where we went shortly after breakfast that first morning: Peter and Andrew and Dorothy and I, though Dorothy sunburned with the slightest exposure, and stayed only for a minute before going back to the room. The rocky ledge above the waves led along at the foot of the cliffs, under the garden walls of villas on the top, and out to the end of the cape, and around it. Some of the rocks were the size of elephants. The flashing green-blue water was transparent. We could see every stone and piece of coral and seaweed on the bottom, ten, twenty, forty feet down. We dove off the rocks into another sunlight.

When we came back Alan was standing on the terrace outside the dining room with a tall, slender, dapper man of about Alan's own age, who looked at once elegant and a little seedy. Alan introduced him as Georges Fratacci. As we stood talking before I followed the others upstairs to change, I was told that Georges was an architect, currently underemployed and working on entries for an architectural competition, and that he was a tenant of Alan's, or a guest of Alan's, or some combination of those that was never stated clearly. He and his wife and daughters were living in the modest, yellow, vaguely neoclassical house across the road from the villa, which also belonged to Alan. We could see its roof from our bathroom window. Georges had a fine-boned, lean, handsome face, set off with a trim Ronald Coleman moustache. He was wearing a pale linen suit, slightly rumpled, and a tie, and two-toned shoes, white with brown wingtips.

He had no English at all, though he had done architectural work, he said, for the American embassy. He alluded to architectural designs on which, apparently, he and Alan had worked together. He spoke to me proudly of being a Corsican. Alan had told him that I wanted to be a writer, a poet, and to Georges that was a clear recommendation. We were both artists. He was staying for lunch, where he would expand upon that theme.

André served us lunch on the terrace, and in the afternoon Alan drove us into Nice. On the way he and Georges pointed out the sights, telling us the names of the villa owners on the cape, and talking of the owner of the hotel and café, the *Voile d'Or,* beside the small harbor. They pointed out the other café, on the *place,* run by a couple they both knew. The wife, as they told it, had come from the demimonde in Toulon or Marseilles, where she had once run an advertisement in the evening newspaper, ending with the phrase "every discretion, near the railroad station." Everyone liked her. Now she was pregnant and the café regulars were looking forward to being honorary uncles and aunts.

We retraced the winding street to where we had turned off the main road the night before, and made our way along the *corniche* lined with bicycle traffic, two and three bicycles abreast, with no intention of getting out of the way of cars and trucks, and then down the steep switchbacks into Nice, our first glimpse of a Mediterranean city, of metropolitan France, of the architecture and civilization of Provence. The traffic was negligible in comparison with what was soon to come, but it was all strange, composed of old cars, wagons and carts, unfamiliar shapes, and so it seemed that there was a lot of it revolving around the white-gauntleted policemen standing at the centers of the principal *places,* blowing whistles. Behind them rose the plain, inherited symmetry of the facades, the sand-colored limestone and harmonious proportions, the rows of shutters—*jalousies*—pale gray or gray-blue or gray-green, reflecting the southern sunlight that had filled the days of the later troubadours and of Dante and Cavalcanti and Petrarch.

Alan had a few routine matters to take care of, calling at his bank and the insurance office. Georges, meanwhile, led us past the big stores and into back streets and older sections of Nice, with overhanging upper stories and tables set outside small cafés in the shade, covered with *socca*—onion and black olive pie. Peter was absorbed by displays of French fishing harpoons, reels, and snorkeling gear. I knew so little that when we came to shoe stores with stacks of rope-soled shoes outside I supposed that the rope soles were a heritage of the shortages of the war years. Georges found us a bookstore. I pounced on the poems of Supervielle and the essays of Camus, an unknown volume of Gide, Valéry's *Monsieur Teste*. (French paperbacks cost little then. They represented a spirit of publishing in which books could be produced cheaply in small editions, according to considerations not hypnotized by the hope of profit. Paperback publishing in the States was still confined to "dime novels.") Alan would raise his eyebrows, of course, when he saw them.

He met us and took us all to lunch in a restaurant on a side street, a place that he had known, he said, all his life. Georges explained the Mediterranean specialties on the menu. We were all celebrating an arrival, only superficially aware of how different the occasion must have been for each of us. To Andrew, who knew no French at all and next to nothing about France, it must have seemed very strange. Dorothy and I welcomed it with blanket and determined approval. Alan, I suppose, was trying to sort out his own plans for the summer and decide how they might include all or any of the four of us. I could see that I was meant to play an important part in his decisions, watching over the activities of Peter and Andrew, making sure they were happily occupied. I scarcely considered that our situation was virtually as new to Alan as it was to the rest of us, and it would be a while before I tried to guess what combination of liberality and loyalties, affections, hopes, and heaven knows what else, had prompted and shaped his idea for the summer.

24

Swimming, walking along the rocks around the cape, and sun-
bathing took up part of most days, especially at the beginning.
Peter wanted us to have underwater harpoon guns. Alan took
us to buy them, and followed directions to a small, dark, upstairs
office in Nice where I filled out a form, sat for a photograph, and
was issued a harpoon fishing license. Peter was too young for one,
but if I had one I could officially be his "instructor." Neither of us
was much good with a snorkel, and neither was Andrew. Dorothy
did not even try. We never speared any fish at all, but for a while
Peter liked to have the harpoons with us when we were out on the
rocks, and we kept them in the cupboard with the yellow inflatable boat, which soon exuded a murky smell of rubber and cats.

One morning we came in from the water to find that another
young couple had arrived at the villa as Alan's guests. Sometimes
he announced such things in advance; more often it seemed not to
occur to him to do that. Alan introduced them as Gilles Quéant—
dark, saturnine, floridly handsome—and his beautiful wife, Françoise, who turned out to be my friend Alain's elder sister. Both of

them, Alan said, were movie actors. I was startled that Alain had told me so little about his family, and especially about his sister.

At lunch, Gilles seemed particularly happy to meet young Americans. He spoke of the world of acting and the film industry in France in a low confiding voice, his model perhaps Louis Jouvet. Françoise and I converged on the subject of her brother and our friendship, which had led me to Alan and France, and she talked a little of their childhood. She was at once friendly, as though we already knew each other, and reserved, giving the impression of being shy rather than wary. Gilles and she might have been riding in different sections of the same bus. There was a glazed distance between them. In the week or two that they were there at the villa, in a room across the hall from ours, he picked up his conversation with me as a continuing thread, easily, casually, in a manner suggesting that we were old friends, and that I knew the main details of this life. I was surprised by his apparent candor, though I was aware at the same time that it was his way of presenting himself, a pose he was rehearsing.

One afternoon, a few days after they arrived, when he and I were sitting by ourselves in the garden after lunch, he asked me whether I was in love with my wife, and then without waiting for an answer told me that he was not in love with Françoise and was not sure that he had ever been, it had just been fun to begin with, in the circles they went around in. It had just happened like that. He described the social and professional world they shared, parties and studios and filming, in a way that was not easy for me to envisage. I was thinking of what he had said about Françoise, and why he would ever have said it to me, whether he was about to divulge affairs of his own, or to describe a marriage in which they both had affairs, or even whether he was about to suggest a bit of wife-swapping. His question, which he seemed to have forgotten was a question, flashed a passing light on something that I knew very well. I was not in love with Dorothy either, but I felt guilty about it, would not have admitted it readily, and was repelled by the thought of announcing it behind her back to someone I scarcely knew, whose possible interest in the subject I could not even guess.

Gilles came and went on his own, into the *place* and on walks around the cape, and he talked at length on the telephone, and continued our after-meal conversations, sitting in the garden. Françoise came swimming with the boys and me. Bikinis still seemed a welcome novelty. We all dutifully tried out the snorkels, and she probably managed them best. Without effort we became friends. She had the reserve that Gilles lacked, and grace, and poise, and she did not tend to talk about herself. Neither of us did that. We did not feel free to, in those circumstances, and there never were any others. Everyone in the villa knew when we were alone together, and we were aware of it.

Georges Fratacci often turned up in the garden when some of us were sitting there after lunch. If Dorothy was there and I was not, he would unfold in his mind the one thumbed, painful sentence of English he could muster, tighten his face and say, "Wear Ease Ure Eyes Burn?" Dorothy managed to understand, after several failures, that he was asking where her husband was, and she would answer in schoolbook French, and I would be called or he would come and find me. Georges would have been happy to include Gilles in his fraternity of artists, but Gilles scarcely noticed Georges.

Georges wanted to show me his studio. He talked of the artist's devotion to his art, his craft, his *métier,* as though it were a quasi-religious vocation, utterly personal and innate, something that the French, he assured me, understood and knew how to respect. He developed the subject as he led me out through the small door set into the big double doors of the villa entrance. We crossed the road to the house set behind a waist-high, yellow stuccoed garden wall and a wooden gate. It was a modest Mediterranean building dating from sometime in the nineteenth century, any time after the Napoleonic era. It was probably much older than the present villa standing between it and the sea. In style it could have been a Palladian gatehouse. The front door opened into a bare, symmetrical hall, with a dining room and kitchen to the right. Georges's wife, a plain, pleasant, withdrawn woman, emerged from the kitchen, and when Georges had introduced me she offered us coffee. Georges led the way after her into the kitchen, where I met their two pretty daughters, eleven and fourteen years old. Georges and I sat down to tins of cookies and coffee, but they waited on us and did not sit down with us or participate much in the conversation. In the days that followed I realized that this was the way of the house, and of Georges's background and perhaps of his wife's too, although I was never sure of that, for I never managed to talk with her by herself. I came upon Georges several times having his meals or a coffee alone at the table in the kitchen, or in the dining room, or outside under the arbor, with his wife or daughters waiting on him but never sitting down with him. I saw, of course, that this was a significant cultural difference and none of my business, but it never ceased to make me uncomfortable, and I observed too that it was a custom that did not extend to other circles of French society in which Georges moved.

In a moment Georges stood up, told me to bring my coffee along, and led the way back through the hall and the evidently scarcely used sitting room beyond it, and with a certain air of caution as though he might be disturbing someone, he eased open the door on the far side of it into another room of the same size, with the blinds of the windows drawn down to the sills, which gave the room a dim, yellow light. He shut the door behind us, raised the blinds, and led me to the long table filling one side of the room. It was covered with a roll of tracing paper, and under that was a drawing board. He rolled back the paper and showed me a long half-finished architectural drawing of a neoclassic facade, with columns, a portico, recessed wings, a wide terrace at one end, trees and bushes drawn in as shadows, darker than the other shadows. Then views from above, from the ends, from inside, and structural details. It was a building design for a competition related in some way that was never clear to me to the American embassy, perhaps for a consular building, and Georges hoped it would lead to a grant and a permanent position, maybe at the embassy itself, all of this with Alan's encouragement. Georges told me that he worked here at night when everything was quiet and he could get the light just right. Sometimes he found that he had worked all night and was still standing at the drawing board when the light began to return through the olive leaves outside the window.

From his studio he led me to the *place,* to the café with its soccer tables, and introduced me to the owners there, the local man risen to proprietor's status, and his evidently popular, pregnant wife *"avec tache."* Then in turn Georges took me to the other café, the more fashionable, expensive, done-up one under its huge awning, on the terrace above the harbor at the *Hotel Voile d'Or.* There the specialty was Guinness stout, either straight or with champagne. At both places, to my embarrassment, Georges insisted on introducing me as an American poet, which the proprietors responded to with polite, perfunctory bows. The *Voile d'Or* host, in brass-buttoned blazer and yachting cap, spoke well-practiced English with an accent from the movies, and told me that he knew another American poet who lived above Monte Carlo, an old man named Robert Service, and asked whether I knew him. He told me that Service came there to the café from time to time, or used to, and that he could find Service's address if I wanted him to. I had just arrived, and was too gauche, green, and snobbish to take him up on it, and have lived to regret that, though in fact it might not have been easy for me to get over to call on the old author of *The Face upon the Bar-Room Floor* even if I had had the address. It was some distance. I had not mastered the few bus routes, and I would not have wanted to go with Alan even if the idea had appealed to him.

Georges on his own had assumed the task of introducing this newfound young American poet to the lore and ways of the arts in the Old World. He sang a few French cabaret songs from Georges Brassens and others, and Corsican drinking songs, not particularly well, in a scratchy voice. One day as we sat on the *place* looking over the water, he introduced me to a French writer of his own age or a few years younger who was shopping for lunch, carrying a string bag that had a baguette, a bottle of wine, a bit of hard sausage, and a head of lettuce in it. The young writer, whose name was Georges Belmont, had rented a house for the summer a few steps away from where we were sitting, and was staying there with his wife and small daughter. He was earning his living at the moment, he told me, by translating from English, which he spoke beautifully. Just then he had a deadline to finish a translation of *The Egg and I*. He invited me to visit him, and made sure I knew how to find where he lived.

Georges Fratacci, for reasons that I had not yet picked up, seemed to be showing me off, as though I were a member of his own family. He began to urge me to go to Paris in the autumn, where he would be working for the Embassy and would introduce me to people who would understand and appreciate me. As he said it I thought I detected a suggestion that Alan perhaps could not be expected to "understand" me, which led me to wonder whether Georges's dependence upon Alan was nourishing his doubts about himself. But I thought of his kindness as an agreeable example of a Mediterranean open temperament, happy to find new, sympathetic company.

25

A few mornings after we arrived, Alan had an ancient Ford, a 1908 Model A, delivered to the courtyard of the villa. The local garage between the *place* and the main road had been keeping it there in storage, up on blocks in the back. Alan walked around it smiling with the pleasure of a child to whom a favorite toy has been restored. I could see that the car represented moments of his youth that he remembered with fondness, from summers when he and his brother had been growing up, but his allusions to those times were oddly featureless and elusive, whether because he realized that they would serve as deplorable examples or because he wanted to keep them to himself, I could not guess. He spoke of the ability to master the peculiar workings and niceties of the archaic vehicle as a new test of my real worth. I suppose I passed, but his attention was on the Ford and he kept to himself any doubts about how practical it would be to have the old car back in the stable again. He had good reason to wonder about such things. By now I no longer remember some of the fine points of coaxing it into action and keeping it awake and tractable, but I recall brass tubing around and under the dashboard, with beautiful antique brass valves, all of which the garage had kept oiled and polished. The main valve controlled the flow of gasoline from the tank to the carburetor, and had to be opened before undertaking the arduous rituals of getting the motor running, which usually— perhaps always—required the use of a crank. Sometimes the operation took two to make it work, one out in front bowing and grunting over the handle of the crank, the other in the driver's seat with a hand on a lever attached to the steering rod, which I suppose was one of the throttles, for there may have been more than one. All this, of course, was before the day of safety inspections. The car had been registered once for all time, and the card was somewhere in it.

Peter had seen the Ford before. He may even have ridden in it, in earlier summers. He now seemed to regard it as an exotic ancestor of the Deer Park jeep, which in a way it was, and Alan allowed him to climb into it and go with me on a tentative sortie along the one road leading past the villas on the cape, where there were no cars to speak of. Peter's hilarity from the summer before, when I had been learning how to manage the clutch on the jeep, came back to him as we inched and chugged out the gate. There were subtleties and protocols to this clutch and gear system too that kept eluding me. For such a simple car the controls were remarkably elaborate, and I did not know whether to ascribe the old car's uncooperative behavior to its age and condition or to my ignorance or to its recalcitrance at having been taken over by a barbarous stranger. Not all of the gears would work, and one of them—I think it was second—liked to change its mind after I had wheeled it into place and had released the clutch, and was driving on, depending on it. It would let me start ahead and then skip back out of engagement again, the motor suddenly racing free with a happy shriek, and the auto's forward momentum, such as it was, dying in one winded exhalation, the wheels giving up instantly. And the brakes puzzled me. They worked, sooner or later, but out of a long sleep, and not always in quite the same way. Still, we made it out to the end of the road and back, and Alan, André, Gilles, and Andrew were waiting in the courtyard to cheer us in, looking a little surprised that we had made it.

What use we might make of the Ford was still not clear. It was kept in the garage by the main gate, alongside Alan's station wagon, and I began to consider what trips it might be used for. I wanted to go to Roquebrune to see the hotel where Yeats had died and the cemetery where he had been buried until after the war, when the Irish navy had sent a small warship to recover his body and take it back to definitive burial in Ireland, in Drumcliffe Churchyard, the place that he had designated. Since my days as a student Yeats had been the modern poet who had meant more to me than any other. I might even get the address of Robert Service and call on him. But I would have to be a bit more confident of the Ford's behavior and my control of it before asking Alan about any such outings.

The real maiden voyage of the resurrected Ford that would determine the possibility of any expeditions in it was to be a drive to Nice and back. The idea must have been Alan's—a ghost from his own heedless youth. Dorothy came along, and he entrusted Peter and Andrew to the Ford's uncertain temperament and my ineptitude. We set off one afternoon in the lull after the midday meal, when the world's drivers, with luck, might still be asleep. André, in his kitchen apron, peered into the garage as we backed out, and as he watched us go, he looked very serious, signaling that he would shut the doors behind us so that I would not have to risk the motor's stopping. We rolled along to the *place,* heads turning as we went by, and up the hill beyond it, with me holding the gear lever in place once I had the auto in second.

There was more traffic on the main road than I had bargained for. The usual bicycles three abreast. Trucks veering out on the curves that gripped the buttresses of cliffs on the *corniche*. I managed to stop at the top of the hill, then lurch and heave forward onto the main road and get into second again. The gear jumped out on the grade, before a tight curve. I managed to get it back in again. The boys were silent. I put on the brakes before the curve. There I learned what their secret had been, back on the empty cape road with no cars ahead of us and behind us. They were really working on only one wheel, the left rear, which meant that if I tried to brake hard or in a hurry the front of the car swung around to the left, toward oncoming traffic. I kept what I had discovered—or I tried to—from Dorothy and the boys. As we approached the next curve, going downhill, I tried the hand brake, which seemed to work, more or less, on both rear wheels, though without great authority. Trying not to slip out of gear when I put the clutch in to brake, I steered us downhill into Nice and managed, in thickening traffic, to negotiate one intersection after another, all the way to the wide open central space where the Boulevard Jean Juarés flows into the Place Massena.

Whatever purpose may have figured in the plans for this trip besides its own dubious self had probably been forgotten by then, and I cannot imagine why I had taken us straight into the heart of downtown Nice, where a constant loud stream of trucks, delivery vans, Vespas, *mobylettes,* and bicycles circled around a policeman on a stand, in a tropical helmet and white gauntlets, directing the current in the middle of the *place.* He, of course, raised his gauntlet in our direction to stop the stream we were in, just as we approached, so that the delivery van ahead of us whizzed on, and we choked to a stop and the Ford's motor shuddered.

When the white gauntlet, with a gesture from a ballet, motioned us on to rejoin the orbiting swirl, I pressed down politely on the accelerator, put the Ford into first, eased off the clutch, and the motor stalled. Horns began jabbing from behind. Staring ahead at the policeman's face above the white glove I tried desperately to start the auto. More horns. Nothing inside could rouse a response from the coma under the hood, and I got out to try cranking it, accompanied by a full brass section. On about the third heave I saw beside my feet several pairs of heavy shoes, and looked up into the faces of two burly figures, drivers of vehicles behind us, who had come to inspect the problem. I gave another heave on the crank but the motor seemed to have returned to a pre-war dream. The carburetor was probably flooded by then. When I straightened up the policeman himself was standing there. I expected some kind of stern impossible command from him, but instead I could see from his face that he was looking the Ford over with a mixture of amusement and admiration, and so were the others. The cars nearest to us had stopped honking, and the continuing chorus had drawn back. The policeman asked me what year it was, and whether its papers were in order. He glanced at my international driving license and nodded. By that time a crowd of drivers had gathered around us and the horns had given up. The policeman suggested that some of the drivers help me roll the car over to the curb out of the way, and try to start it there. Dorothy and the boys got out, and half a dozen of us wheeled the Ford aside and let the stream flow on. The first two drivers on the scene, who had assumed a proprietary role in the Ford's performance, had it started in a moment. Then, after a question or two, they restrained their curiosity with evident difficulty before trotting back to their own vehicles, whose motors were still running as they sat like islands in the current of traffic.

We made our way cautiously into a relatively empty square, parked, explored some of the narrow streets of old Nice, found a tiny dark restaurant where we all had *socca,* and then went back and coaxed the Ford awake again and groped our way out of Nice, up the road to Italy, back to the villa. Alan looked surprised —perhaps he had not noticed until then that we had all gone. He asked how the Ford had behaved and I told him about the second gear and he nodded. He remembered. It all came back to him, he said. Then the brakes. I told him their shortcomings and he agreed that they needed some work if the Ford was to be driven at all. He had the man from the garage come and pick it up, and it remained in his keeping for the rest of the summer.

26

The owners of the few big villas out on the cape all knew each other, more as colleagues than as friends. In Alan's demeanor with regard to them, and in his introducing me to them, I could discern again the screened mixture of feelings—of kindness, reticence, uncertainty, obstinacy—that I had come to recognize but not to understand. The neighbors were often not in residence at the same time, he explained, and they had never been intimate, and in recent years had become still less so. But the servants, the skeleton staffs of the villas, knew the family gossip of each place and it had long been common lore among them. André and Georges, and eventually Josephine, were eager to entrust me with more and more bits of gossip about the past of Alan's family, beginning usually with his mother's drinking bouts. Josephine showed me the enormous bathroom that Madame had designed for herself, a room the size of her bedroom, but with the walls and floor covered in white tiles like a shower. A huge bathtub, a chaise-longue. There she could lock herself in for a week at a time and drink. And, Josephine said, sometimes throw the empty bottles out the window where they sailed past the garden, down onto the rocks below, and Joseph would go down and try to collect the pieces. Her drinking habits seemed more memorable and outlandish to them than any of the family's scandals involving sexual pranks. Things of *that* nature seemed to be taken quite for granted. I could only guess what the neighbors actually knew about each other, and what each knew that the others knew about Alan's and his brother's escapades in earlier years.

Alan took me next door to meet the American owner, explaining that they had some matters to settle about a shared wall. A Chinese doorman, in Chinese attire, met us at the gate and showed us up the steps to a living room where much of the furniture consisted of big Chinese pieces. The owner greeted us, accompanied by a large, beautiful, cream-colored Chow. The man was older than Alan by a decade or so, not especially affable, obviously used to having his own way. The Chow was reserved and suspicious, of Alan in particular. We sat down, and drinks were served, but from the start the conversation did not go happily. The problem about the shared wall, and the drainage from the tiles along the top of it, was stuck before it really started, architecturally and perhaps legally. Both of them spoke of possible legal recourses, and the tenor of impatience rose. Before long Alan stood up to go, both of them making an increasingly unsuccessful effort to control their tempers, and the Chow watching closely. The man accompanied us to the front gate, with the Chow between him and Alan, his attention on Alan, but not making a sound. As we stepped out of the gate Alan said to the neighbor that those dogs had been used for food in China, which was all they were good for, and the door slammed behind us.

On the other side of the *Villa Cucia Noya,* along the cliff toward the middle of the village of St. Jean and the *place,* was the Singer villa, topped by a tall, stone, Italianate tower. No one had been in residence there that season. A skeleton staff—gardener, housekeeper, janitor—came and went, and in the first days there it remained closed to us, behind its high wall. Beyond it, around a curve in the road, was the arched entrance to the Vanderbilt villa, with wide grounds enclosed by a lower wall that one could see over. It was a gingerbread castle in off-white stucco, its current form perhaps a product of the twenties.

Alan knew the current occupant, an aging American tycoon whose name I am afraid I have forgotten. The man had been there since before the war and now was in residence much of the year. He had become a citizen of Monte Carlo, a Monegasque, to avoid American taxes. Just after the war, however, when the American forces were more or less in charge of the area, he had claimed privileges as an American, and had been surprised when they were not readily granted. Alan took me along to call on him.

A succession of liveried servants (the men were dressed like the delivery boy in the Philip Morris advertisements of the period) led us to the entrance hall, full of sunlight filtered through two-story stained glass windows. Our host, a short, puffy, intense man in a light gray suit, received Alan affably, telling us both that he had just finished his daily French lesson—he was really determined to try to speak it properly, after all these years. Then, as a servant was taking our drink order, he began to tell Alan about what he had been doing by way of restorations to the villa, which he said had suffered more from the German occupation and withdrawal than any of the others along the cape. He stood us in the middle of the entrance hall and asked Alan whether he noticed anything. Alan looked around to try to see what he was supposed to recognize, but he was not left to guess. The proud *chatelain* pointed to the largest stained glass window, at the end of the hall, the size of something over an altar in a big church. Its central figure was a knight in full armor, gazing and striding upward.

"Sir Galahad," he said. "As you remember." Then he reminded Alan of the cement blockhouse that the Germans had built down on the rocks below the villas, with its guns trained on the coast across the bay. And as Alan knew, he said, when the Germans were retreating from Italy and moving north they had blown up several of their fortifications along the coast, and that was one of them. He himself had been in Monaco at the time, of course, but when he came back to the villa he was appalled. The effect of the blast had been terrible. It had all but destroyed the Sir Galahad window. But he said he had managed, with great difficulty, to have it completely restored, this time with his own motto—which he pointed out—incorporated in the design.

Alan and he sat and discussed what could be done about the *boite de nuit,* the source of *La Vie en Rose,* that had been installed in the bay below the villas, and they went over the history of its materializing there while they had been looking the other way. They reviewed what they understood of the local politics, deals and debts and favors, that had allowed it to happen, and the influences and names that might be enlisted to get it removed, though neither of them thought that was likely to happen before the summer was over. They commiserated with each other about the disgrace to the cape and the nuisance to guests. And speaking of guests, our host told us of a lunch he was having for the Duke and Duchess of Windsor, and a group of their friends, in a week or so (we had already heard about it from Josephine). He murmured something about not having realized that Alan had arrived, and about an invitation, but it was clear that his plans were satisfactory as they were, and Alan waved the suggestion aside, and came away smiling about the visit, and happy to have escaped the luncheon party.

But some of the social life of the cape began to swirl around us as the summer *fêtes* approached. A classmate of Alan's, and fellow member of the New York Racquet Club, moved into the villa of a mutual friend, and came by for a drink with his blonde, plainly anxious wife and their pretty, very blonde, extremely shy daughter who looked like a life-sized doll. Mrs. McCormick (of McCormick harvesters) came with her own beautiful daughter, Muriel. It was no secret that Mrs. McCormick had her eye on a titled English bachelor for Muriel, but it did not prevent either of them from being generally friendly, and Mrs. McCormick was happy to find company of Muriel's own age.

Somerset Maugham, whose white, imposing Villa Mauresque loomed over the end of the cape, came to drinks with several young men who were on his staff. When he held out his fingers to be shaken, looking elsewhere the while, I had never felt a living hand so cold, loose, and limp. He looked even older and more tortoiselike than Graham Sutherland's portrait of him. I remembered my mixed response to his writing, when I had read it in college a few years earlier, and I listened for him to say something—anything—but apart from a few syllables croaked or whispered to his young men, he said nothing at all for general hearing.

André, in his white jacket, served at these occasions. I was aware of a shadow of resentment that came and went with him. André and his wife had not been there for long, whereas Joseph and Josephine were part of the architecture and history of the place, and seemed to know everything about its past. André was not happy in his own relation with Alan. The way Alan spoke to him, and ordered him around, abraded him constantly. His marriage seemed sullen too, and his wife kept to herself, but he said she was not happy there either, and he was not sure they would stay when the season was over.

Joseph kept to his garden, which seemed to be a whole world to him, though he had a way of appearing whenever anything was needed. He and Josephine looked rather like brother and sister. They were well past middle age, gray, very thin, dressed mostly in black or gray. Josephine was the old soul, the feminine deity, the Inanna of the villa, and she had not forgotten or dismissed the lures of youth. She thought André's marriage was hopeless from both sides, and she was not on intimate terms with him or his wife. Her tone about Alan suggested that he came and went as he had always done, and she did not expect much of him. His present setup seemed to her agreeably quiet, and she hoped it would stay that way. She must have concluded that neither my own marriage with Dorothy, nor Gilles and Françoise's marriage, was a carnival, and she took an interest in my swimming and sitting on the rocks with Françoise, whom she admired, and assumed that I must too. If anything further had happened between us, however disruptive it might have been, it would have had her sympathy and approval.

And why did nothing happen? The goldfish-bowl circumstances in the villa, the proximity of everybody to everybody else, no doubt had something to do with inhibiting it. Or was the spark really not there, in fact? The question returned, of course, when it was too late ever to be sure about anything to do with it.

After the first week or so at the villa, Alan left for a few days in Paris, one of his absences that, like his departures from the Deer Park the summer before, were usually mentioned no more than a day in advance, and nothing else was said about them to any of us. They were none of our business. He was back before the summer *fêtes* began, but we did not participate in the *Fête des Lumières* in which families on the cape, and each of the villas whose owners were in residence, generally paid a handsome subscription to rent a fishing boat for the evening, complete with crew and adorned from stem to stern with hoisted lanterns. One by one they were rowed out in a long wreath of boats around the harbor. The lanterns included the big, bright Aladdins with reflector rims that were normally hung on the bows of the boats to attract squid to the surface at night. Each of the subscribing families was announced in turn over a loudspeaker, the names interspersed with loud, festive music. There were speeches by local officials, broadcast in the course of the program, and then fireworks and more music. Alan had sent a donation, but instead of taking part we sat on the terrace of the *Voile d'Or* and watched as the families were heralded one by one, and boarded under the bobbing lights. We were watching as the loudspeaker announced "Dooblavay Mawgaset Maugam *et famille*" and we saw him totter onto the craft supported by a ring of hands from the crew and his *famille*. Alan's friend from the Racquet Club, and his blonde wife and daughter, were announced as they teetered aboard another lantern-lit fishing boat, helped by shadowy arms. We sat staring as the fireworks rose over the drifting galaxy of lights in the bay between us and Beaulieu. Later, when the boys were in bed, the party continued at several of the villas, more and more crowded, bibulous, and chaotic. At one point, in the Vanderbilt villa, I came upon the wife of Alan's Racquet Club friend sprawled on the red-carpeted stairs, helplessly drunk and in floods of tears. Her daughter was in the room below. Alan had seen his friend's wife too, I learned as we walked back to the villa soon afterward. He attributed her trouble, as though he had private knowledge, to some inadequacy in their sex life.

27

The *fêtes* with their lights, music, parties, crises, and hangovers comprised the traditional succession of events on which the summer season was strung. They were close enough together to create an accelerating rhythm of their own. Before one of them, not long after the *Fête des Lumières,* Alan planned ahead for us more elaborately than he usually did. He arranged to take us all out for the evening to dinner at the *Abbaye* in St. Paul de Vence. That would include the two boys, Georges Fratacci, Gilles and Françoise, Dorothy and me. We fitted tightly into the station wagon and set out in the summer twilight.

That was the evening when Alan, at an intersection, pointed to a road north that we were not taking, and mumbled to me that up that way was where he had been dropped by parachute to join the Resistance, and where Jean Prévost had been ambushed and killed. Françoise was sitting in the seat far to the rear and almost certainly did not hear him mention it, but it was not a moment to go on asking about it.

The *Abbaye* is a handsome ancient building set into the rocky outcrop and cliff side on which the village had grown during the Middle Ages. Alan and the proprietor greeted each other like old friends. Alan said the place had been a favorite haunt of his family's. We went on a short walk around the building and its gardens and environs, with Alan pointing out architectural details that he admired, and then settled under a pergola for drinks while our dinner was being prepared. The terrace where we sat overlooked the coastal plain of Provence, all the way to the sea, and as we sat there the lights came on out of histories of their own. Alan was in an expansive mood, in animated conversation with Gilles, by the time we were called to dinner.

We had trout, as I remember, and excellent wine, white and red, Alan introducing Dorothy and me to local vintages that he knew would not be familiar to us. The dinner was unhurried and festive, at ease, familial, and taking its own way like a ride down a gentle slope with hands off the handlebars. We sat talking around the table, and Alan was in no hurry for the evening to end. When he came back from paying the bill he announced that he had reserved a table for us at Maxim's in Cannes, and as we bundled into the car I wondered whether it was safe for him to drive.

Maxim's turned out to be another place where Alan and his family had been known for years, and the *patron,* or the presiding figure that evening, greeted him warmly and welcomed him back, and we were shown to a couple of tables at the edge of the dance floor, where the show was due to start in a little while. It seemed to me that the boys might be a little young to be taken to a nightclub, or to be allowed into one, but I consigned my doubts to provincial inexperience, and sat at a table with them and Dorothy. Alan ordered cokes for the boys and champagne for the rest of us. The floor show began.

There were ballroom dancers: tangos and more tangos. Innocuous family fare. And comedians talking much too fast for me to understand. The boys were not interested. Peter and Andrew were whispering about something else, probably miles away. Alan was getting through the champagne. I saw with concern that the second bottle was almost empty on his table when the others had scarcely finished their first glasses.

The featured performer of the evening turned out to be a transvestite, apparently a local celebrity, to whom the comedian referred with modulated awe and innuendos that I did not catch but that made the audience laugh. The program built up to his act, or acts, which included singing, dancing, and comic routines of his own. His introduction was set off and punctuated by fanfares from the band. The lights dimmed slightly, and in the beam of a spotlight the star came on, in a ruffled red evening gown, wearing red pumps with high heels, and began a camp, falsetto comic patter interspersed with bits of increasingly suggestive dancing. Alan turned in his chair and called loudly to order more champagne, which the waiter brought, and opened, as discreetly as he could while the act went on, and Alan went on drinking.

The singing became more sultry and suggestive, and Alan began to heckle the performer, at first muttering in clearly audible disgust, and then beginning to call out insults as the dancing continued. At first the boys appeared to think Alan's interruptions were funny too, a kind of accepted audience participation perhaps, and then I saw that Peter was disturbed and frightened. The others at Alan's table, Georges and Gilles and Françoise, looked helpless, and Alan obviously was in a very ugly, drunken frame of mind. The waiter stood watching. Alan's insults got louder, and it sounded as though the band was trying to drown him out. At what was meant to be a dramatic moment in the dance, as the band built up the climax, Alan suddenly heaved himself onto his feet and, shouting obscenities at the dancer, flung himself onto the dance floor trying to lay hands on him. Instead he fell onto his face and lay there while the waiters leapt forward to help him to his feet, and to restrain him, and Georges and Gilles and I stood up to get him under control. He fought off the waiters and snarled at the rest of us, but then allowed himself to be led toward the entrance desk.

The *patron* or *maitre d'* calmly took charge. He and Alan managed to settle the bill, and then he and I agreed that Alan would need somewhere to stay, and he called and reserved a room for Alan at the Negresco. He said it was the hotel that Alan's family had used, over the years, in Cannes. Alan glared furiously at me and at the rest of us. Rather than have us try to get him into the Jeep station wagon, the *patron* called a taxi, and got Alan into it. I elbowed Georges in with him, and the rest of us got into the station wagon, and I drove after the taxi to the Negresco. Peter was trying to control his tears.

Outside the hotel we left the boys and Françoise and Dorothy in the car, while Georges, Gilles, and I walked in with Alan, who kept warning us in a kind of low growl to let him alone, swearing at us, mumbling something about having been a boxer in college. He did not want any of us to go up to the room with him and the bellboy, and we watched them advance on the elevator, with Alan trying to walk straight. Georges and I explained to the head clerk what my relation to Alan was, and I asked for, and was given, a second key to Alan's room. I was assured that it was a particularly quiet room.

I wanted to get the boys out of the whole thing and back to the villa. Somebody would have to stay there to be around when Alan woke up. Georges said he would come back with me. The others elected to stay there in the lobby. With Georges beside me and the boys silent in the back I drove through Nice to St. Jean Cap-Ferrat and tiptoed into the villa with the boys, then turned and went back.

By the time we got to Cannes and the hotel, the night was nearly over. Dorothy, Gilles, and Françoise, in the lights of the avenue, had gone across to the beach to lie on towels. But the head clerk told me that after they left there had been what he called a little drama. Alan had rung for room service and ordered champagne. When the bellboy brought it and opened it, Alan asked him to draw him a bath, and when the boy came back from the bathroom Alan had already knocked back a glass or two. He flung his arms around the boy, trying to drag him into bed. The boy had struggled, as tactfully as possible. He had been told that Monsieur was an important guest. He had managed to escape, but he had bolted from the room without turning off the bath. He remembered that, a few minutes later, but did not dare to go back in alone, and he rounded up two others from the night staff to go with him. They found the room empty, the bottle nearly empty, the bath still running and overflowing, and the bathroom floor already an inch under water. They searched along the corridors for Alan and found him wandering half dressed, hopelessly drunk, looking for the bellboy. With some difficulty they herded him back to the room where he collapsed into bed again and fell asleep. There they had left him, not long before we returned.

We decided to let him sleep for a while, if he would, and to have some breakfast, and then to try to get him home in the course of the morning. Georges stayed in the lobby, stretched out in his linen suit, exhausted. I went across the avenue to the beach and found the others. The stars were fading, to the south, and the first pallor had seeped into the eastern edge of the sky. They sat up one by one, stretched, and we picked up the towels to go for a walk along the sand.

Not far from us, along the water's edge, some fishermen were preparing to haul in the net they had laid out past the breakers at the beginning of the night. We got into conversation with them. They wanted to know where we were from. We asked whether they would like us to help them haul in the net, and after some polite demurring they accepted the offer, warning us about getting wet and fishy. Gilles and I rolled up our trousers, and we left the towels and shoes up past the high water line and all waded in with them to pick up the haul ropes, and in the sound of the small waves curling and breaking around our legs they shouted instructions to us, and when they told us to we began to pull.

It must have taken us longer to bring the net in than it seemed. The last stars faded as we hauled together. One of the fishermen began to sing and the others joined him. We pulled to the singing and to the shush of the waves crumpling and sliding out from under us. The net broke the surface, and the bright loom before sunrise glinted on the flipping silver curves caught in it as the long weight inched upward out of the water. Then it was up at the waterline, out of reach of the ebbing waves, and we saw the whole struggling catch quivering and gasping as the rays of the first edge of the sun, startling us with their warmth, touched it with light.

We all let down the ropes, and the fishermen began to open the net, peeling it back as we watched. They started to take the fish out one by one, sorting them into big baskets. They offered us our pick of them, but we thanked them and said we had nowhere to cook them. "Take some home," they said with the sun red on their faces by then, as they hurried to lay out the fish for the morning market. We stood there in the sunrise with them for a moment and then said good-bye and walked back along the sand.

Georges was asleep in his chair in the lobby. He said Alan had called to order more champagne but the hotel had made excuses and had not sent him any. As far as anyone knew he had gone back to sleep.

We all had coffee and croissants there in the lobby, and then ordered another pot of coffee to be taken up to Alan's room, and Georges and Gilles and I accompanied the waiter. There was no answer to the knock on the door. I tried the key and the door opened and we all went in. Alan was in bed, half asleep, groggy and in a rank mood, not wanting to see any of us, then or ever. Georges and I, in both languages, told him that we had brought him some coffee, and that it was time for him to get up and get dressed and go home. At last he managed to push himself up into a sitting position and take a cup of coffee and begin to drink it, saying nothing. Georges poured him a second cup, and he drank some and mumbled something to Georges about having a shower and getting dressed, and for Gilles and me to wait downstairs until he was ready.

Gilles and I went back down to wait, and eventually the elevator doors opened and Georges and Alan emerged, Alan looking as though he had been carved out of soap, and they walked to the desk. The bill was ready and Alan settled it. I brought the car around to the front of the hotel and we got in. Alan rode beside me in front, saying practically nothing all the way to the villa, where André met us, hovering around Alan to help if necessary, but as Alan started up the red tile stairs in the main hall he turned and snapped at André, "I'm perfectly well, thank you," and went on up alone.

In the evening a taxi came to take him to Nice and the night train to Paris.

28

Gilles and Françoise left a couple of days later, and the villa was very quiet that evening. André and Josephine spoke with concern, and undisguised curiosity, about what had happened that night. Peter had told them that Alan had suddenly become sick and we left it at that, but it was not a convincing tale, especially in view of the atmosphere of embarrassment that lingered around it, and Alan's immediate departure after he got back. In the next few days, while other events took precedence, both André and Josephine found moments to extract some of the real story.

The day after Alan left, Georges Fratacci, Dorothy, and the boys and I went into Nice, and Georges showed us bits of the town that we had not seen, and we had lunch, scarcely referring to what had happened. The trip to town had been thought of partly as a way of distracting the boys. Peter and Andrew said almost nothing. When we got back, André met us with an ashen face. While we had been in town that morning and both girls were out of the house, Mme. Fratacci had tried to kill herself. She had taken sleeping pills, and when the girls came home they had found her unconscious and hardly breathing. They had called the ambulance, which had taken her to the American Hospital in Nice. It seemed very likely that she would not live. The girls had gone with her.

I drove to the hospital with Georges. He rushed to the entrance desk and told them who he was. His wife was in a cool, green room, the shades drawn, in an oxygen tent, white and waxen, but she was breathing, although one had to watch closely to be sure. The girls were sitting by the bed, as they had been since they had got there. They were distraught, and Georges sat down with them, stunned and wordless. I stayed with them for a while and then talked with the nurses outside the room, who were guarded with all details, including her chances of survival. Not a word from anyone by way of explanation.

Evening came on, mealtime approached. None of them wanted to leave. Georges said they would be all right. He would take care of them at the hospital. I asked him whether there was anything he wanted me to do at the house. Then I told him that I would be back the next day, and left.

She was at the hospital for another two days, gradually reviving, and finally Georges brought her and the girls home in a taxi, and they helped her inside. Still nothing was said about why it had happened, except for Georges murmuring once, absentmindedly, "I was not paying enough attention."

That was the situation Alan returned to a day later. He was carefully shaved and dressed and looked as though he had just been discharged from somewhere. It was impossible to say how the sequence of events since the dinner at St. Paul de Vence had worked on him. He was quiet. He seemed neither surprised nor particularly disturbed by Mme. Fratacci's suicide attempt. He did not seem to attach much importance to it, besides making sure that she had whatever medicines and care she needed. He asked

Georges about her medical situation and left it more or less at that. He said he was sure she would not want visitors, and Georges agreed. At meals he was distant and polite, but it was impossible not to be aware that his demeanor was covering a depth of barely contained anger.

One morning Peter and I took the small, inflatable yellow life raft out onto the bay and managed, after many attempts, to rig the mast and sail so that it would actually move with the wind. The breeze was from the villa side at that hour, and the shallow craft, with no keel or leeboard, slipped sideways as it went, taking us off-shore toward Beaulieu. We dropped the sail, and as we started to paddle back I saw Alan, up at the wall of the villa's garden, waving angrily, and realized that he was summoning us to come back. I was reminded instantly of the times in my childhood when I had managed to escape for a moment and play with other children, only to look up and see my father waving to me to stop it and come to him to be scolded. When we got back Alan was furious with me. The air might have escaped from the inflatable boat. We could have been drowned. Peter's face darkened and he walked into the house, while Alan continued to upbraid me for taking such a risk. We should have been wearing life preservers, although there weren't any. Mrs. McCormick and Muriel were coming for lunch and Alan managed to produce smiles for the occasion, but she could not have failed to notice a certain awkwardness. Mrs. McCormick said she had heard about the troubles with "your tenants"—she meant Mme. Fratacci, and directed a passing inquiry in that direction.

In the next days Dorothy and I were moved across the road into the smaller villa where the Frataccis lived. The beautiful big room overlooking the garden and the bay toward Beaulieu was one of the main bedrooms of the villa, and Alan explained that Maria Antonia would be coming before long and it would be needed for her. He kept his own rooms in the tower because they had been his rooms in his youth, and because they were on a floor by themselves.

The quarters in the other villa lacked the elegance, space, and views of that first opulent room, but they were quiet and off by themselves, and there were in fact several rooms that became ours, including one that I could use for reading and writing. I had with me my pocket editions of Villon and Nerval, my Hill and Bergin anthology of the troubadours, and the six small Temple bilingual volumes of Dante. I was immersed in reading back through the *Purgatorio* just then. Dante compared the crags of Mt. Purgatory to those at La Turbia—*La Turbie,* which I could see towering behind Beaulieu—and when I looked across I imagined him seeing those cliffs from some point along the coast, and noticing them clearly, so that he remembered them later. Thomas Mann's *Doctor Faustus,* which I had read just before we left for Europe, echoed in my head all through that summer. Two or three of the poems that would go into my first book had been written, and I was trying to hear something new, on my own. The upper rooms in the small villa were a place where Dorothy and I each had a place in which we could settle and read, when Peter and Andrew were occupied with something on their own.

One afternoon Alan said he would like to go to Monte Carlo that evening, with me. It gave him a chance to disparage my clothes, which was easy. I certainly possessed nothing that could pass for evening dress. I do not remember whether his invitation included Dorothy. Anyway, she did not come. She did not have evening clothes either, and she had been afflicted by asthma ever since our arrival, the symptoms not acute but recurrent, and so had spent much of the time there in bed reading. She would probably not have wanted to go to Monte Carlo, and Alan would not have pressed her to.

He said he knew a waiter over in Beaulieu who he was sure

would lend me a dinner suit that would fit me, and early in the evening Alan, in his dinner jacket, drove us over to Beaulieu, where the waiter was expecting us, with his suit, including shoes, socks, and a black bow tie. I changed in the waiters' bathroom in back of his restaurant, while Alan and he stood talking, and then we set off for Monte Carlo.

Alan led me to the summer casino, which he said he thought I should see. He had telephoned ahead and arranged for us to be met by the director, a Russian prince whose name I failed to grasp. Alan told me that the prince had been a general under the czar but had lost his estates in the revolution. He and his family had escaped with nothing. We were met by a very tall, imposing, white-haired gentleman who welcomed us and led us through the casino, not yet crowded at that hour, though there were small, intent clusters of addicts around some of the gaming tables. The prince spoke to us both in French, as though he were confiding in us as particular friends, or leading us through a conservatory in some country house of his. He had been, in fact, a friend of Alan's parents, and had known Alan as a boy, before he occupied his present position. He offered Alan a drink, and we sat in his small glassed office for a few minutes, where the two went through the minuet of inquiring about each other's lives since they had last seen each other. Then Alan said that we were on our way to dinner, and they assured each other that they would meet again soon. As we left, Alan spoke of the old prince fondly, but alluded to White Russians in general in a way that made them sound undependable and possibly contagious.

He had reserved a table for us in the restaurant upstairs, where the windows looked out over the yacht basin to the sea. There was a band platform. Tables were set around a dance floor. At one table I recognized Eric von Stroheim, Merle Oberon at another, and there were other familiar faces, American and French, from the film world. Alan greeted some of them, and friends at other tables. Several diners stopped to speak to him as they arrived. His conversation was with them, or in his own mind, but scarcely at all with me, and again he began drinking hard, starting with vodka cocktails before he went on to wine. He kept speaking to friends of his at nearby tables, rather awkwardly, and I could hear his voice rising. He was growing irritable, short with the waiters. I found it difficult to talk with him, to keep him on any subject except for the diners that evening, the famous faces, what he knew about them and about others whom he had seen there in the past. His bits of anecdote became more and more incoherent. The headwaiter came over and asked how long he had been at the villa this summer and how long he was planning to stay. Alan rumbled in reply, pleased but disconnected. He began to talk to himself or to some imagined adversary, so that it seemed he was not addressing me or anyone nearby, but heads turned toward us as his voice rose. He called for the bill and said we would leave before the dancing began. He stood up, staggered a few steps, with everyone's eyes on him, and half collapsed, breaking his fall by grabbing the back of a chair, which tipped over onto the floor. A waiter and I helped him to his feet and over to the entrance desk, where he settled the bill. The car was sent for. He managed to get down the stairs, gripping the rail, sullen and silent. Fortunately I did not have to grapple with him to keep him from trying to drive back to the villa. When we got into the front hall he started up the stairs, swaying perilously but muttering to me to keep away from him.

That night marked the end of the season for him. I drove over to Beaulieu the next day and returned the waiter's borrowed evening clothes, and told the waiter that we had had a fine evening. It seemed to me when I got back that the villa had entered another age. Alan paid little attention to what happened there. A young woman named Effie Halsey, an art student, daughter of a friend of Alan's, whom I had met at the Deer Park the year before, came for a few days' visit and was troubled by Alan's demeanor and by the atmosphere of the villa. She talked about Alan's mother and brother, their ruinous behavior resurfacing in the present. She was acquainted with people cruising on sailboats moored in the harbor, and we went out sailing some days, with Peter and Andrew or by ourselves. She sailed down the Italian coast with one of them, and after she had gone Alan left on trips and was away for days at a time.

By the middle of August he was talking about leaving, and about Peter's return to the States to get ready for the school year. Other guests were expected. Alan arranged for them to stay at the villa whether he was there or not. Josephine and André took care of things in the house. Maria Antonia da Braganza, who had engaged me to come to Portugal as a tutor to her two sons, was expected before long, and Dorothy and I were to stay on at the villa until she came. There was not enough left from my small salary during the summer for us to do any travelling in the meantime.

The day came when Alan's and Peter's bags were packed into the Jeep station wagon for the drive to Paris. In spite of Alan's disruptive, ill-contained core of anger and the unappeased urges that fuelled it, he had tried to be generous and kind, not only to Peter and Peter's shy and often bewildered friend Andrew, but to Dorothy and me, and in the course of two summers a mistrustful, troubled affection, a dubious, ambivalent rudiment of family feeling, mottled with resentment, had grown among us. It was as evident in Alan's valedictory behavior as it was in our own. Of course he was saying good-bye to something besides us, to some aspect of his life, some hope, and his gesture was waving to something beyond any of us, and we could feel that too. Peter seemed to be angry about going, and he got into the car and looked away, and they drove off down the road.

29

The days that followed were a kind of interregnum, a time apart, filled with an unmoored, indigent freedom, and with quiet and room. André served us our meals at the villa, out on the terrace as before, but he lingered to talk. I sat in the kitchen gossiping with Josephine, trying to imagine her own youth, not far from there, and the German occupation, which she remembered vividly. I had a room to try to write in, day after day. An Austrian-born physician, Alan's doctor in New York, had been invited to spend a few days at the villa. He came with a tall, willowy young English woman, his current girlfriend. They settled in easily, entertained themselves, and were agreeable company. Mrs. McCormick, who was staying nearby, came with Muriel and took us on an excursion to Éze, and to lunch at La Réserve de Beaulieu, and afterward to visit her friend Lord Beaverbrook at his villa. On another afternoon she took us to Juan les Pins, and to Antibes and the Picasso museum, and to see Nicholas de Stael's paintings.

Downstairs from our rooms at the small villa, Mme. Fratacci recovered gradually. I sat in the kitchen with her, a few times when

I saw her there and she asked me in. She was a very quiet woman, staring at a prospect of loneliness, but though she was somber she was not depressing. Her daughters were attached to her like shadows, too timid or too withdrawn for me to be able to coax them into conversation of any kind. Georges neglected his wife and knew it, and seemed unable to imagine doing anything differently. He sat at the kitchen table and had nothing to say to her either in French or in the Nizzarte patois that was her childhood language, and which they had usually spoken when they were alone together. The kitchen, filled with helpless good intentions, would rapidly become suffocating, and if Georges was there he would get up cautiously, as though he were afraid of stepping on something, and lead me out. We would walk into the village, with him talking, perhaps, about Alan and his problems, or about his *métier*, the world of the arts, Giacometti, Cartier-Bresson, but never about his own life and marriage.

By the time Alan left I was calling almost every day at the tiny house that Georges Belmont had rented for the summer months, overlooking the inner bay of the cape, between the thumb and the palm. The principal room of the house was the everything room. An unmade bed occupied most of it, with Georges's typewriter on a kind of card table in a corner, by the door to the bathroom. Georges's wife, José, was often there when I arrived, in her underwear, smoking. She was never not smoking. Georges allowed gaps between cigarettes, but often worked with one smoldering in the ashtray beside him. José had a low, hoarse voice that would have been attractive if what she said had not been almost invariably pejorative, caustic, discontented, and impatient. Her chronic disappointment was directed at Georges, not for any specific shortcomings but as the habitual tenor of her address to him. I found her hard to be around from the beginning, but fortunately she spent as much time as possible down at the beach with their two- or three-year-old daughter, Sophie, in the little sandy cove just below, and when she left, Georges and I could sit and talk. Those days inaugurated a friendship that would last, despite José's abrasive accompaniment and my own peregrinations during the years that followed, for over half a century.

Georges's English was fluent, grammatically flawless, with a ready, precise, rich vocabulary. It was English, but American English and American writing were certainly not alien to him. His barely noticeable French accent enhanced its charm. He had learned English as a student, perfecting it at Trinity College, Dublin, where he had been a schoolmate and close friend of a young man named Samuel Beckett, who at that time was known chiefly for his first book, a critical study of Proust. Georges talked of his friend Sam, and of Joyce, during the years when Sam had acted as a kind of secretary for Joyce in Paris, and the three of them, for some time, had met almost daily. Sam, he said, had taken to imitating Joyce in many respects—small mannerisms, turns of speech, Joyce's walk and clothes. Georges noticed that he had picked up Joyce's physical hesitancy that was a result of his eye trouble. Then he could not help observing that Sam's feet were bothering him, to the point where it was painful for him to walk, and that the condition seemed to be getting worse. He brought up the subject with Sam, who at first dismissed it, but finally admitted that he had been wearing shoes the same size that Joyce wore, and they were a couple of sizes too small for him.

For a while, Georges said, Joyce had wanted to go, every Sunday morning, to one particular church, to Mass and to sit through the sermon. They had not been sure why, and had even wondered whether the creed that had surrounded his childhood was exerting its claims, years later. Every Sunday after Mass they would go to a café and sit drinking white wine, and Joyce tended to be quite silent at those times. He would sit with a cigarette between his lips, the ashes dropping off and rolling down his front. It went on for weeks, and then one Sunday, at a moment when they were sitting there saying nothing, Joyce raised his head and began a tone-perfect imitation of the priest's delivery, phrase by phrase, the manner, the rhetoric, the argument and exhortation flawless. The performance, besides filling Georges with admiration, had led him to ponder how it could be that the imitation was so much more compelling and alive than what it was imitating.

(Two years later, when Georges was living in a villa at Villescresnes, just south of Paris, I stopped to see him, and while I was there Beckett came over. It was the day of the publication of *Molloy*, and he and Georges were feeling celebratory. Beckett had been told that there were to be some good reviews. José told him confidentially that she quite liked the book but was "not convinced," as she put it, by his French, which she said he wrote like a foreigner. And then she went out somewhere, and Georges suggested that the three of us make gazpacho for lunch. Beckett was given the job of slicing the cucumbers. I watched him with something approaching amazement. His slices were so fine they were all but transparent, and they were perfectly consistent from one end of the cucumber to the other. Years after that I wrote to him from London. I had been asked to put together a program of contemporary poems for the BBC Third Programme, and I greatly admired the few poems of his that I had seen and wanted to know whether he might have others that had not been published. In my letter I said that he probably would not remember me, but that we had met at Georges's house, and the three of us had made gazpacho. I told him how I had admired his slicing of the cucumbers. He wrote back that, as far as poems were concerned, the cupboard was bear [sic], but that he did indeed remember that day, that lunch, the cucumbers. "I was thinking," he wrote, "about my mother.")

Georges had also become a close friend of Henry Miller's and had translated several of his books. He knew a good deal of contemporary American fiction, both literary and popular. He was a modest, gentle, hardworking man, who was trying to use his long hours of daily translating to buy himself a little time to work on poems and a novel of his own. I felt that he was somewhat at the mercy of his circumstances, his marriage among them, though he dealt with them without complaint and with a steady flow of energy. His mind, his perceptions, the language in which he expressed himself, were fine, authentic, and judicious, but he seemed to live with an ultimate doubt of himself, to suspect that he was a shadow of others.

A friend of his, renting another small, brand-new dwelling on that side lane, was an Irish novelist named John Lodwick, who had been in that part of France during the war as a clandestine operator for the British armed forces. He had been parachuted into the region to maintain contact with the Resistance and to assist in sabotage against the Germans in the late stages of the occupation. While there he had met Jeanne, a beautiful, already ravaged woman, who said little but obviously possessed a powerful character, and lived with a deep rage, which John ascribed to her experiences during the war, when she had been raped by the Germans and had seen them murder several members of her family. He said that she had been able to take it out on several of the Germans before they left, but that had scarcely soothed her or reassured her about what life had to offer. He had fallen in love with her just the same, the moment he met her, in the Resistance, and had returned to her as soon as he could. They had a little boy named Malachi, still in his crib.

John liked his red wine at all hours of the day. Usually he did not show the effects of it until near sundown, when he was apt to be preoccupied and irritable. He had published some short fiction, and a book about amphibious commando operations during the war, which had received a good press and some success, and he had carefully assembled a large scrapbook of press cuttings, which he liked to display. It was the one object to which he seemed particularly attached. All three of us loved the writing of Joyce, and talked of it, and about Joyce himself. John shared my fascination with Camus and Mann. He had not yet read *Doctor Faustus* but had been reading about it, and knew the central story, and asked about the book. At one point he wanted me to say whether, if—like the composer who was the protagonist of Mann's great novel—I had been offered a period of years of artistic fulfillment in exchange for something I thought of as my soul, I would have accepted. I was startled by the question, and answered that I thought I would have had difficulty believing in the "devil's" offer at all, and the authority for making it. I thought that if the talent and urge and character were there to begin with, such a bargain would be meaningless. If they were not there, no "bargain" could help. John seemed troubled by my answer and I could not tell why, but there was something about him that suggested a man possessed and struggling with forces that he could not control.

These took the form of recurring violence, a theme of violence in his life, and occasional glimpses of it in his demeanor and his expression, like the fin of a shark. It was there in some of the stories he told, and he told them at all hours of the day, sometimes starting, apparently, out of nowhere, and when he told them I could not help but listen. Many had to do with the war, the clandestine operations against the Germans, which had filled several of his most formative years. They told more often of escapes than of encounters or confrontations or moments of engagement. More than once, according to his accounts, he had made his way out of France, across the Pyrenees into Spain, after completing operations for which he had been sent into the region. Once, he said in a story that he returned to and that clearly haunted him, he had got to the border near Andorra and had run out of money. A man there, who he knew worked in the black market, lent him some, to get him over the border. His creditor was taking a long chance, but John was planning to be back. The man was a Jew, who hoped to escape also, before he was caught, and would need the money, he said, to be able to buy his way out if they did catch him. John did come back on his next trip and learned that the man had lost the gamble, had been caught and deported, and John felt a complicated, ineradicable responsibility for it, and was sure that the man had not escaped sooner because he did not have the money John had borrowed from him.

On one of his trips out, John said, he and two other men were escaping by foot over a high pass. They had been hiding by day, travelling at night, for most of a week. One of the others was a man with whom he had been on missions before and knew relatively well. The other one had joined them later. They did not know much about him, he was not much help, and he kept getting on their nerves. They told each other that he was only too likely to make some stupid mistake and get them all caught. They were short on sleep and food. John and his friend found that they really did not like the other man. They saw it in each other, in the way they watched him and referred to him, and they admitted it to each other with their eyes, and eventually with words. Up on the high trails they began to wonder how far they trusted him. They decided to get rid of him and call it an accident. They picked a moment at night, in a high wind, and at a precipitous ledge on the trail they pushed him over.

So John said. I wondered, though, not always at the time but afterward, how many of John's dramatic stories, or what parts of them, were true, and how much of them he himself believed.

He told me one about Yeats, whose poetry he knew I carried with me.

Yeats had died on the 28th of January, 1939—"disappeared in the dead of winter," as Auden wrote in his elegy. He and his wife, George, had been staying, that winter, at the Hotel Idéal Séjour, on Cap Martin near Roquebrune and Menton. Yeats's health had been failing, in stages, for years. At St. Jean Cap-Ferrat, just over ten years after his death, with the war having come and gone in the intervening decade, I thought of what I had read of the accounts of his life and death in the biographies that had been written by then. I had an image of a hotel up on the mountain at Menton, and of his last days alone up there with his wife. But the Hotel Idéal Séjour, which George—Mrs. Yeats—had found a year earlier, and where they had spent the winter before, was in fact a quiet *maison de repos* dedicated to such winter retreats. They had much of the villa, and its garden overlooking the sea, to themselves, and Yeats was surrounded by friends, some of whom were spending the winter nearby. They included Dorothy Wellesley, and Hilda Matheson, Walter Turner, Desmond and Mabel O'Brien, and Yeats's last paramour, Edith Shackleton Heald. Several of them were present on what Auden called "his last afternoon as himself."

Yeats had known for years that his time was limited, and he had told his wife that if he died there at Cap Martin he wanted to be buried in the nearby cemetery at Roquebrune, and then a year later dug up and taken to the one at Drumcliffe near Sligo, in Ireland, which he had named in the poem *Under Ben Bulben*. He had hoped that the delay would allow him to escape an Irish public funeral of the kind that had been organized for his lifelong friend, the writer George Russell. Yeats was buried according to his wishes, at Roquebrune, but before the year was out France and most of the rest of Europe were involved in World War II, and his body remained at Roquebrune until September 1948, less than a year before the summer when we sat talking about him across the bay. By then the age before the war seemed to have been gathered into a remoteness like that of the classics.

But John told his story about "last year," when the Irish navy had sent a corvette, the *Macha*, to Villefranche Harbor, just west of St. Jean Cap-Ferrat, on the way to Nice. According to John Lodwick, one of the *Macha's* officers had been driven to Roquebrune

for the ceremonial removal of Yeats's coffin, and while there had
visited an old Irish lady who had been in Roquebrune all through
the war. She had been deeply disappointed, John said, when the
officer's gift to her, after those years, had been neither Bushmill
nor Jameson whiskey, but a box of *tea*. While the visit and the ceremony of removal and the journey with honor guard from Roquebrune to Villefranche were going on, others of the *Macha's* crew,
John said, awaited the funeral cavalcade beside the small harbor of
Villefranche, where there were convenient cafés, and there they
had sampled the local products, and were well primed by the time
the cars wound down the steep hill and drew up beside them. So
well, in fact, that although they managed, with some difficulty, to
load the coffin onto the waiting launch, when they got out to the
corvette and were engaged in hoisting it aboard they bungled it
and the coffin fell into the water and had to be fished out and
bound securely before it could be swung onto the warship.

Even at the time, I thought John's tale remarkably reminiscent
of the coffin accident on the way into Glasnevin cemetery in
Ulysses, and I tried to find out whether others had heard it, and
whether or not it might be true. I was in Villefranche once or
twice before I left, that summer, but no one seemed to remember
it, though it sounded like something that would have become legendary in no time. Eventually I inquired about it from several
Yeats scholars and was assured that nothing of the kind had taken
place. (R. F. Foster's magisterial *W. B. Yeats: A Life,* volume II,
Oxford University Press, 2003, tells us as much as we may ever
know on the subject.) There had indeed been some confusion at
the time of disinterment. When Edith Shackleton Heald returned
in 1947 to the site of the original burial, she could not locate it. It
turned out that the graveyard authorities had granted a conces-
sion for the grave for ten years (George Yeats had a receipt), but
they had thought it was for five. The local record had been lost,
and apparently the church officials had put the grave in a part of

the cemetery owned by the township, in which as a general rule the leases were only for five years. At the end of that time they had exhumed the remains and put them in an ossuary. The French government was called in to sort the matter out, and they officially identified the remains (though how they did that we can only guess) and placed them in a new coffin, which was delivered with due ceremony to the Irish representatives in September 1948 for the return to Ireland. Rumors about the confusion spread at the time, and John may have heard some of them and improved upon them in his own version.

Between Alan's departure and Maria Antonia's arrival, when we had the villa more or less to ourselves, my college friends Bill Arrowsmith and his wife, Jean, and Bruce Berlind and his first wife came for a visit. There was room for all of them in the small villa where we were staying. We went to Nice and explored the town. Bill grumbled and argued and was brilliant and difficult. His passions at the moment were Eliot and Pavese. He had extended his classical learning to include modern Italian, and he was already working on his translations of Pavese's poetry and talking of that most powerful and memorable of Pavese's prose books, the *Dialogues with Leukó*. Bill was several years older than I was, and as students and graduate students we had been constant sparring partners, but I had learned invaluable things from him, mostly about modern poetry and the classics. Before I knew Bill he had been one of Richard Blackmur's first protégés, and prodigies, and he had been one of the founders of the literary magazine *Chimera*. He was jealous of his early eminence and anything or anyone whom he considered a threat to it. He detested and ridiculed John Berryman, and many of Berryman's contemporary enthusiasms, from Auden, MacNeice, and Spender to Delmore Schwartz. I remain grateful to him for first leading me to the poems of Wallace Stevens, and for insights into the play of syntax and what it could render possible in poetry, which he had come to from his studies in the Greek and Latin classics, and which I could confirm in my reading of the poems of Yeats and of my other great early enthusiasm, Milton. But Bill was as cantankerous a companion in France as he had been at Princeton, and his responses were grudging and carping about most things, from the architecture of this degenerate post-Latin culture to most of the days' activities. Bruce, on the other hand, has always been a peaceable man, and he spent much of his time trying to calm things down. Bill's humor could often be improved by steering the conversation to subjects he was fond of, such as the music of Handel or the writings of Samuel Butler, whose notebooks he loved to quote. It would be years before our long association eased at last into something we both felt sure was friendship.

One moment sets that interlude in the context of history at large. Dorothy and I are sitting in the café on the *place* at St. Jean Cap-Ferrat, with the Arrowsmiths and the Berlinds, unfolding the newspapers we have just bought there, and we learn from the headlines that the Russians have the bomb. The days of the cold war had begun. We sensed it as we sat there.

30

It was not very long before Maria Antonia arrived in her big dark red Buick convertible, with her small boys, Anthony, eleven, and Robert, seven, and her niece and nephew Johannes and Mafalda von Thurn und Taxis, from Austria, who were roughly my own age. At once we moved into a different reign, the final metamorphosis of that summer in the villa. The big living room seemed to come to life, with its tapestries on the wall and its view of the long garden at the far end, and of the bay, Beaulieu, and the crags of La Turbie, from the French doors along the side. When Alan had been there we had gathered in that room occasionally, but Maria Antonia seemed to make it her own—her sitting room, conference room, reading room, coffee room. The hall was full of the sound of people speaking other languages on the telephone, as Johannes and Mafalda and Maria Antonia talked to family and friends in Vienna and Paris, Lisbon and Monte Carlo. Maria Antonia arranged to settle in at the villa, while at the same time arranging to leave it and set out on the next stage of her trip back to Portugal.

The old White Russian prince who was the manager of the summer casino at Monte Carlo was a friend of hers. (I had not understood his name when Alan introduced us, and failed again to catch it when Maria Antonia mumbled it, and I did not get her to repeat it, so I never was sure of it.) She called and scheduled a meeting with him, and she and the boys and Dorothy and I drove over to Monte Carlo to see him. He and his beautiful, white-haired wife received us in their apartment in the hotel above the casino, where the windows looked down into the yacht harbor. His wife prepared tea in a huge samovar. He was writing his memoir. A volume or two had already been privately published. He showed us the large bound volumes, removing them carefully, like cases of butterflies, from a shelf in a tall armoire in which his dress suits and uniforms were hanging. The volumes contained hand-painted portraits of the principal characters. The old prince had a reputation as a portrait painter, and I believe some or all of the paintings were his own. Over tea Maria Antonia made arrangements for him to paint portraits of her children, starting with Anthony. I was to bring him over every afternoon to sit for an hour or so. It became a routine that continued through most of the time that Maria Antonia was at the villa. After the first day or two, whoever rode over with us—Dorothy, Roberto, sometimes Johannes and Mafalda—went to the casino swimming pool while Anthony, and later, Roberto, were having their portraits painted.

Johannes and Mafalda pored over the French and Monte Carlo rotogravure tabloids filled with gossip about the titled figures of Europe, their engagements, weddings, divorces, and above all their scandals of every variety. They seemed to know most of the principals and to know all about the others, with an intimacy that combined high-school social politics and the devotion of collectors. Their interests appeared to be comfortably contained within the margins of these sepia-printed pages and the current kaleidoscope of the *Almanac de Gotha*.

Maria Antonia was in her middle forties. She had probably never been a great beauty. She had a rather dumpy figure that was thickening with middle age. But she was direct, decisive, kind by nature, with an easy grace and magnetism. Her voice was deep, throaty, with a very slight accent in English. She spoke French, German, and her native Portuguese with equal ease, and she treated me, from the beginning, with an air of special confidence, expectant but bounded, that seemed to assume a kind of friendship. If it was a manner, it succeeded with me. We sat and smoked together—the slender cigars that she preferred, which were sent to her by admirers from two continents and the Canary Islands—and I told her, cautiously at first, about the summer with Alan. The details of it seemed to sadden her but scarcely to surprise her. She spoke of Johannes and Mafalda as a couple of children, though Johannes, I think, was actually a year or two older than I was. That allowed me to see, or to guess, another reason why she had wanted to have a young American tutor, even one as ignorant of Europe and as devoid of social experience as I was, for her American-born sons. Her European Almanac de Gotha upbringing and background, which I was just beginning to glimpse, was fundamental to her life and outlook, but her marriage to Alan's New York cousin, and her years in the United States with her children, her divorce and later independence there, had revealed to her another outlook entirely. Her children were half American, at least, and she did not want to have them deprived of that side of their life.

It was the European side of her, the Braganza side, that was more apparent at the villa. She talked on the telephone with the Comte de Paris. There seemed to be some chance of his coming south while she was on the *côte*, and of their seeing each other. In the end it did not happen, that time. Too bad, she said. She told me I would like him. The rumor of her presence had spread, perhaps from friends at Monte Carlo, and among other invitations one came from a Princesse de Beauharnais-Lichtenberg, who had a villa over in Beaulieu. She and Johannes and Mafalda talked about that one, whether to accept it and go over to tea or drinks, or not. Maria Antonia's older sister, Filippa, who was the titular head of the Portuguese monarchist party and far more fundamentalist in her approach to all such matters than Maria Antonia, certainly would not have accepted because the Beauharnais-Lichtenbergs bore an upstart Napoleonic title. Johannes and Mafalda were very doubtful about it, and rather in favor of declining. Maria Antonia accepted, for all of us, and drove us over to Beaulieu, found her way through side streets to a small, upright, urban villa with a fixed, frosted glass awning over the front door, where we were received by a pleasant, reserved woman in her late thirties, who might have been a kindergarten teacher, and her all-but-silent mother, both of whom curtsied to Maria Antonia. We had tea and cookies, the edges of a conversation, and it was all friendly, stiff, full of good intentions, and without direction or prospect.

Johannes and Mafalda discovered the pedal boats down at the nightclub below the villa (officially boycotted, of course, when Alan was there) and they spent hours pedaling around the cove. Maria Antonia went on organizing the trip to Portugal. The luggage for all of us was a problem. There was too much to fit in the Buick. We conferred with the French railroad office about train tickets for Dorothy and me, from Nice to Coimbra in Portugal, and learned that it would require a complicated journey with several changes of train, in France, Spain, and Portugal, and it would be far more expensive than if we all went by car. I suggested a trailer for the luggage, and Maria Antonia liked the idea. It seemed to appeal to an adventurous, deliberately unconventional streak in her. I went down to talk to the local garage man who had Alan's ancient Ford in his keeping, and he said that he had just the thing out in back. It had come in the day before, after the summer trips:

a nearly new car trailer, the right size, with metal sides and a hatch back. It should take all our trunks, and the cost of it was considerably less than the price of two train fares, with luggage, to Coimbra in Portugal. He would have to weld a trailer coupling onto the rear bumper of the Buick. I was not sure whether the princess would like that, but when I told her she seemed to think the idea rather dashing, and she and I took the Buick down to the garage and walked back to the villa. The *garagiste* delivered the Buick the next day, with its new trailer, and showed Maria Antonia and me how to uncouple it, with the cables connecting up the trailer's brake lights and signals to the Buick, and how to couple them again. The car and trailer sat waiting in the courtyard on the gravel from then until we began to pack them, on the day before we left. The trailer transformed the Buick into a piece of wanderers' equipment, a reminder of things to come. Maria Antonia seemed to like having it there, as though it were a costume for a future event. Josephine referred to it, without inflection, as a *roulotte,* a gypsy wagon.

By then we were well into the month of September. The Fratacci family had left a week or so before. Georges Belmont and his family were about to leave for Paris. The weather, and the light on the *côte,* were more beautiful than ever, with a shade of amber at the days' ends, and the mornings cool. I had grown fond of Josephine, with her unsweetened perspective and her affection, and of Georges Belmont and his company. I felt sure I would come back, and they would be there.

We began to load things into the trailer a few days before we left, and we finished packing it on the morning we were going, in the cool, gray first light, our footsteps sounding loud on the gravel, and the long trimmed walks of Joseph's garden echoing as we went back and forth. After we had made final trips around our rooms to make sure we had left nothing essential behind, André and his wife, and Joseph and Josephine, gathered to see us off. The big car was crowded when we rolled through the gate and down the road and along the coast, westward, to Marseilles, where we stopped for lunch, and then on to Foix, in the Pyrenees, where we spent the night.

The next morning on the terrace outside the hotel, sitting over coffee with the mountains around us, the taste of the bread, the smell of the woods, the shadows on the peaks, remain vivid many years later. That day we drove on and crossed the Pyrenees into Spain, a moment of great excitement for me. Spanish was the first European language I had tried to learn, and the landscape of Spain was the first part of continental Europe that I had tried to imagine. I felt a link, expectant and possessive, with the country of the Spanish *romances* and the poetry of Manrique and Lorca and Machado. Whatever I saw of the country was resplendent by definition.

Long stretches of the main roads in northern Spain had not been paved but simply graded, and we drove more slowly than we had in France, although often for miles we were the only car, the only vehicle on the road. Maria Antonia preferred to do most of the driving. Johannes urged her to let him spell her, and occasionally she did, but she was not completely at ease unless she was at the wheel herself. We drove through long valleys on the southern side of the Pyrenees as the first light of autumn reached them and the colors deepened. We stopped for a rest in the shade of oaks and then drove across the rolling plains of Castille, by vast pastures full of dark cows and fighting bulls. As the sun began to go down we stopped, north of Burgos, in a wide landscape filled with the orange and red westering light before sundown. The light was in our eyes, and it was a good moment for a break, to walk along the road and watch the massive black shapes wading slowly in the ember of day, and talk of what we had seen in two days. The early September daylight lasted very late. It was getting on for dinnertime even in Spain. We got back in the car and drove toward

Burgos. It was just starting to turn dark when Maria Antonia reached to put her sunglasses away in her handbag and found that she had no handbag. Then she remembered that she had put it on the roof of the car, with the sun still in her eyes, and had forgotten to pick it up when she got back in. In the bag was all her cash, her passport and driving license, Johannes' and Mafalda's passports, Antonio's and Roberto's passports, as well as everything else she might have wanted to have at hand.

The police station in Burgos was like a dingy hotel, the walls painted a swampy green some time before the Spanish Civil War, but despite her lack of either money or documents of any kind, and the fact that she knew almost no Spanish, and Portuguese was not a reliable substitute, she seemed to have no trouble convincing the senior police officers of her identity and what she was doing in Burgos. Apparently there had been some publicity about the family of the pretender to the throne of Portugal being allowed to return to their country after years of exile. The officers were respectful, deferential, said they would dispatch a car immediately to where the bag had been left, and would report to the hotel. They telephoned the hotel to explain what had happened. We went over to register and they were waiting for us, as though the mishap conferred additional eminence on the princess and her party, and we were shown to our rooms. It was around ten o'clock by then. We had expected dinner to be over by that hour, especially as we had heard that a new law about meal hours had just been passed in Spain. Spanish meal hours, the government had decided, were ridiculous, and in the interest of efficiency or of conformity with the habits of visitors whom they hoped to have, the evening meal in public places was to start no later than eight or nine o'clock, I forget which. Apparently the edict had passed like a small cloud. No one seemed to take it seriously. We were invited down to dinner, and as we entered the dining room army officers and their families were being seated at the same time.

Before dinner was over the headwaiter came to the table with a message for Maria Antonia, and when she stood up we saw the chief of police waiting in the doorway. They had found her handbag and wanted her to verify its contents. A peasant walking along the road had picked it up, probably only a few minutes after we had left, in the twilight, and had hailed the police car when it came along. Two other officers were waiting with it, out at the desk. Nothing in it had been touched. Maria Antonia changed some money at the desk, put several bills and a note of thanks into an envelope, and asked the police officers to promise to give it to the man who had found and returned the bag, and to be sure to tell him who she was, and repeat her thanks. She thanked them in turn, and they responded with bows and clicking of heels and sweeping of hats. It would be a local legend for a while.

I would have loved to see something of Burgos, the Burgos of the Cid, but Maria Antonia wanted to get to Portugal, and we headed west early the next morning, across the broad landscape. She planned to spend that night in a government *parador* in Ciudad Rodrigo. The *paradores* were a new provision for the tourism the regime hoped was coming, now that the country's borders were open again. Ancient, noble buildings, castles and great houses, had been carefully restored and converted into handsome, comfortable, impeccably run hotels, sacrificing as little as possible of their ancient grandeur.

Ciudad Rodrigo, until then, had been simply a name for me, a key point in the border wars between Spain and Portugal, and between shifting alliances in wars of succession between brothers who were heirs, or claimed to be heirs, of the kingdoms of Castille and Portugal. I read more, as we approached it, of the bitter feeling that still lingered there, almost a century and a half after the Napoleonic occupation of the peninsula: memories of cavalry stabled in churches, of horrors such as those commemorated by Goya. I learned that greyhounds were considered indigenous to the town and wandered through it freely, some of them belonging to no one, and fed, haphazardly, by the inhabitants, as mascots of the town. I suspected cruelties behind that fairy tale, but I would not learn the truth of it—dogs dying of abuse and starvation, dogs hanged from trees—until years later.

It was a small town out on the upland, facing the mountains. In some respects it looked as though it must have changed little since the army of Napoleon left. The outskirts were walled compounds with open space, greens, stretching between them, through which the band of bare road had been worn by ancient use. Across the greens greyhounds roamed singly or in twos and threes, shadowy, elegant, neither wild nor domesticated, from no age. The greens narrowed to cobbled streets and a town scarcely bigger than a village, without any of the scars, deformities, and visual cacophony of the industrial age, no billboards, signs, cement, or machinery. We reached the *parador,* an ancient fortress, in mid-afternoon, walking in through the tunnel-like entrance in the massive wall, at the top of a rise that may have been part of the fortifications in earlier centuries. Inside, the stone and plastered walls, and the light reflected from them, were cool, and the building was full of echoes.

We had time, before dinner, to wander through the streets of Ciudad Rodrigo and gaze at the large, ancient, stone houses, none of which seemed to have been built later than the sixteenth century, many of them bearing, at their corners, huge stone heraldic blazons, the crests of their families. Each was a small palace. There were ancient churches in the town, and others, some of them empty and in ruins, standing in greens at the edge of it. The whole site held something of the atmosphere, the distance in the present, of a museum, and it was not easy to tell how much of that quality was due to recent restorations, and how much to the town's remoteness, its worn antiquity. It must have been a summer retreat for a few ancient families, for generations. Out on the green, voices reverberated from behind walls, the sounds drifting with the scent of burning charcoal, out of the unknown past.

The next morning we drove on toward the mountains, the Portuguese border. There it seemed to me that Maria Antonia, upon showing her passport, was received with a mixture of careful formality and hesitant deference, as though the head officials were not sure whether it was a good thing to let the royal family back into the regime of Salazar, their employer. They waved us on, to Guarda and the wooded mountains of Portugal, the Sa da Estrela. Johannes and Mafalda kept correcting each other's English, without recourse to those of us for whom it was our native language. "Oh look," Mafalda said, as we climbed through the forests. "Veelets." "They are not veelets," Johannes said. "They are wyelets." Here and there the forests appeared to be ancient, magnificent remnants. Sights of gorges, mountain streams, low at the end of summer. For Maria Antonia it was increasingly familiar ground.

31

The afternoon was growing late when we came to the valley of the Ceira, east of Louzá. As we made our way along the valley Maria Antonia grumbled about the eucalyptus trees that had been planted there a generation earlier. They were a fire hazard, she said, and they had replaced the original forest and now nothing else would grow around them. There were groves of them here and there on the slopes just above the road, but there were mimosas along the stream, and the scent of their flowers drifted through the long bronzed light in the valley. As we turned at the bends of the road we could see the small river flashing over rapids. A narrow bridge, and then the village of Serpins, tacked along both sides of the road. There were people on foot, some of them barefoot, oxcarts with solid wooden wheels screaming out as though in pain as they turned on the axles. A train station with a small train waiting. Green locomotive and passenger cars, with polished brass trimmings, from the first years of the century. Stacks of firewood along the tracks to fuel the locomotive. Then the road out of the village, up the river.

The valley widened to include small fields and orchards, an irregular patchwork hemmed with old walls, a few figures out in them, dark cows and sheep moving slowly, and their shadows reaching across the low amber crops. We came around a corner and saw, far up the valley, a farmhouse set just below the road, to the left of it, and below it the roofs of other farm buildings, and beyond them a tall water wheel, turning slowly like a ferris wheel at a carnival, all of them shining, bathed in the westering light.

To my surprise Maria Antonia stopped the car so that we could look at it from there. That house below the road was the one where Dorothy and I would be living, she said. It was the old farmhouse of the Quinta Maria Mendes (pronounced *Minj*). Somebody produced a camera and took a picture, and then we drove on and stopped in the road, four steps above the front door.

From the way the road passed the house it was apparent that it must have been simply a track for oxcarts, until recently when it had been graded and widened for use by logging trucks going up and down the valley with loads of pine trunks from the government plantations on some of the slopes. The trucks, as we would learn, went by infrequently—one or two a day, and sometimes none. I unlashed the baggage in the trailer, and as I did, a sharp-featured young woman in a black dress and a black-and-white checked apron opened the front door below us and came up the steps, and a young man in a green livery jacket and chauffeur's cap followed her.

She curtsied to Maria Antonia and said, in a high, shy voice, barely audible, that she was Quitas. "Oh yes," Maria Antonia said, and turned to tell me that Quitas would be taking care of us and of the house, and she introduced us. The young man, Martin, was her chauffeur, and they had been expecting us. Martin insisted on carrying our footlocker trunks into the house to the bedroom. Maria Antonia showed us through the rooms.

It would be hard to guess the age of the farmhouse. It must have been patched, repaired, added to, altered, for centuries.

Some parts of it may have been there, along the Ceira, since the age of Henry the Navigator. It was part of the estates of the Comte de Feijo, a prominent monarchist with large cotton interests in Angola, who had lent the quinta to Maria Antonia for as long as she wanted to stay there. She would be over at the new house, which he had built across the river. We could just see it, up among the mimosas. I was happy to be down at the old farmhouse.

The front door opened into a main room, with a new brick fireplace on the wall facing the door, and a window in the deep wall to the left, with shutters folded on the sides and a window seat below it. Another room off it to the right overlooked a farm courtyard with a well in the middle, stalls for animals on the ground level, and storerooms off a wide porch on two sides of the courtyard, above them. The courtyard led out through a deep tile-roofed arch, its massive doors standing open.

Beyond the front rooms, another main room, with a dining table and chairs and another new brick fireplace, and a bedroom off to the right, and then a hall with more bedrooms on either side, and at the end the rudimentary bathroom, with an iron wood-stove, and a window looking down to an outer barnyard, an orange grove beyond it, low barns, and a small but massive building by the river that I would discover was a mill. The kitchen was one flight of stairs down from the dining room, on the ground floor, off the courtyard, and I saw that in the warm months some of the cooking had been done on charcoal braziers outside, but Maria Antonia told us that Quitas would bring us our meals from the main house, across the river.

Maria Antonia and the others drove on around the farm compound and over the bridge, and we explored the house and unpacked. To me the building seemed palatial. The recently rebuilt fireplaces had semicircular hearths extending out over the broad, cupped, and cracked floorboards. Otherwise everything in the house was of indeterminate age. All the windows, set in the deep walls, had window seats, and heavy shutters above them. The furniture dated from at least a century earlier, the time of Eça de Queiroz perhaps. The beds were great solid plateaus, and the bedclothes were coarse linen, under the hairy striped blankets that I would see in the markets. They were covered with white crocheted bedspreads. Looking down into the courtyard from the room off the living room, or the bedroom, was like looking down into the Globe Theatre, with the whitewashed porches and storerooms around two sides of it, like galleries. Bunches of drying beans and strings of garlic and onions hung from the outer beams of the porches. There were no attempts at adornment, except perhaps for the huge flattened heads of the studs on the heavy doors in the roofed entrance. Almost nothing in any of the rooms, on any wall or patch of sunlight on the cracked plaster, spoke of a particular moment in the current of time that had flowed through them. My life had had no part in any of it, I had never set eyes on it, I knew only a few words of the language, one of the languages, that had been spoken there, and yet standing there, walking from room to shadowy room, sitting in a hard chair listening to the house, felt like a homecoming.

As Dorothy unpacked and settled in I went downstairs to the kitchen. There was a vast old black woodstove, and by the door there were deep laundry sinks. Even in the warm September afternoon that was still part of the wide margin of summer it was already sunless and dank down there, with a chill to it, and to the courtyard outside. I went out through the open door. The place was still a working farm, as I would discover in the days to come. Feathers of chickens and ducks, and their droppings, and those of sheep and goats, littered the courtyard and the cobbled area outside it. A tall basket of potatoes was leaning against a post. A wooden bucket stood upside down on the rim of the well. A lamb's fleece hung drying on the balcony like a small child's garment. No one was around.

I walked out through the arch into the open barnyard. Over hatch doors in a nearby shed I could see the heads of cows, sheep in another. I peered into the mill door and listened to the rush of the millrace somewhere below, stepped in and saw the thick beam that was the axle of the millstone, broad as a big table. It was an immense log carved and shaped, the center of the press. A smell of jute, of crushed olives and fermentation, and of dashing water. Two men in dark clothes and black hats were in the courtyard when I came out, on their way to the cowshed. They nodded, touched their hat brims, mumbled monosyllabic greetings, and were gone, as though they saw me there every day. I walked down into the orange grove along the river. Turkeys were wandering in the glowing, late, dappled light that made the oranges blaze like signals. Through the trees came the rushing sound of the river on its stones, and the scream of the tall water wheel turning, upstream from the bridge, and the bubbling gossip of the turkeys, a hen announcing herself somewhere, the mumbles of the men in the shed, and a silence of evening coming on.

Of course I wanted to have the whole language of that place revealed to me, the history of the farm, of the house, the occupants, those who had worked the mill and planted the orange trees and tended the animals and built the water wheel. I wanted to be able to converse with those who were living there. I had felt repeatedly, as we had driven across western Spain and the Sa da Estrela, along old walls and the outskirts of peasant villages, an intimation of the profound continuity of the peasant world, which I caught sight of chiefly in the structures that had been evolved by it, for its physical purposes, by hands and lives that had long since vanished. Remnants of walls, stone steps, shelters for animals represented a current of existence that was older than any of the chronicles, or any of the great names of the ruling families. The current was still alive around me, and there again at the quinta I felt it, like the passage of a migrant bird.

Quitas came down across the bridge bringing us lanterns. I strained and tormented my few words of Portuguese to try to talk with her. She wanted to show us how to use the lanterns. They were beautifully made of cut tin, with four glass windows set behind curved tin arcs. One of the glass panels, in its tin frame, opened on hinges like a door, and inside it a round tin container the size and shape of a biscuit held a wick that led down into the olive oil inside. She told me that a man in the village made them, and he sold them, besides, in the fairs. We should have these here, she said, and they would give us others besides when we came back down from the new house after dinner. She had come to show us the way.

I managed to gather these scraps of information from Quitas with some difficulty and many mistakes, punctuated by her occasional smothered giggles, with her apron stuffed into her mouth. She was as baffled by us, of course, as we were by her. She was shy, merry, somber—generally somber—and inscrutable by turns, like a small merry-go-round, her sharp, thin face with its long nose and high cheekbones lighting up, then darkening and returning to a fixed melancholy, her eyes seldom meeting mine. She seemed even more suspicious of Dorothy than of me. I could not guess whether that was a result of personal chemistry or because she was used to turning to men as figures of authority.

She led us out, not through the kitchen door, downstairs, and across the courtyard—the way she came and went, herself—but through the front door and up the steps to the road, and along to the recently graded turn toward the river, over the broad cement bridge that could not have been there for more than a few years, and up to the main house that appeared to be about the same age, so that I was led to wonder whether the Comte de Feijo had actually had the bridge built so that he could build the house, or whether he had used his influence with the government to get it built where it would be most convenient for him. Quitas led us to the front door and then disappeared around the house. Maria

Antonia told me later that Quitas worked in the kitchen, and that she had come that summer from a peasant family up in the mountains, and had never worked indoors before.

Maria Antonia wanted to know whether we really liked the house, and she had some presents for us, to put into it: tablecloths and napkins, and some local pottery. Candlesticks, a set of rough black coffee cups and saucers made locally. She introduced us to a young woman named Annalisa, a cousin from Austria, who was fluent in Portuguese, and in English and French, and was there to serve as her secretary. In the big main room of the house, with a row of windows onto a glassed terrace and the river below, a long table had been set. There were tall candles burning on it and large vases of flowers for a dinner to celebrate our arrival. The cooks and servers had prepared a feast, and Maria Antonia seemed pleased to be pouring Portuguese wines, a variety of them, some sent by the Comte himself for the occasion. We all talked of the trip. Annalisa and Maria Antonia went over details of the house, speaking in Portuguese and German. Annalisa and a housekeeper had been there for several weeks putting things in order. Annalisa's father was in Lisbon and was due to return in a few days. (I met him then: a frail, gentle old prince, whom everyone regarded as something of a saint. He had been a hero of those Catholics who had opposed the Nazis in Austria, and had spent several years in a prison camp, where he had not been expected to survive. His self-effacement in the prison, in his efforts to help other prisoners, had become legendary.) Maria Antonia and Annalisa talked about him at dinner and afterward, as we sat smoking cigars, watching the night deepen over the river and the roofs of the farm and the steep pine-covered mountainside beyond it. We sat there by candlelight, and then the servants brought in kerosene lamps. There was electricity, supplied by a generator, but they used it only when they really needed it, and all of the servants were country people used to living with lamps and lanterns at night.

Maria Antonia poured out *aguardente* in liqueur glasses for

Johannes and herself and me. The decanter of it, she told me, had been left for her as a present by the Comte, and she was giving me a bottle to take down to the farmhouse. It was nearly white alcohol, stronger than brandy, aged for a while in wood but still firewater, with a woody taste. She explained to me that it was made there on the farm, from the fruit of the arbutus, the strawberry bush, which grew wild all over the mountains. The fruit was a round, dark red berry with a slightly sweet, musky taste. The berries were edible, but I was told later that its Latin name, *Arbutus unédo,* suggested that one should eat no more than one of them. They were reputed to have all sorts of effects, medicinal, cathartic (especially), and even toxic. Maria Antonia loved the taste of the *aguardente*—in small quantities, she said—and we all sipped it as a kind of initiatory draft.

Maria Antonia began to talk about the Sa da Estrela, the towns and monasteries, Viseu, the Mondego valley, Coimbra. One day soon we must go to Coimbra. I could see that she was allowing herself, cautiously, to be happy to be back in Portugal.

She had one of the women from the kitchen light the lanterns for us and show us how to do it ourselves, and we said good night outside on the terrace and started down the drive to the bridge, surrounded by the rushing note of the river and the night scent of the mimosas. In the yellow light of the lanterns even the raw cement bridge seemed to have life and a story. From the middle of it we stood listening to the turning complaint of the water wheel, and the Ceira flowing beneath us, under stars brighter than we could remember. Then we walked on, accompanied by the sound of our own footsteps on the empty road, to the smell of old wood as we opened the front door of the farmhouse.

Quitas brought us our breakfast early, everything under napkins on a round tray. The local bread, *broa,* baked at the house, was a heavy, gray loaf, the flour part corn meal. It had a flat potatoey taste that I liked—but then, I was disposed to like every new thing that appeared before me, if I could. The gritty coffee came in a pot of black crockery. Quitas had a fire going in the woodstove downstairs to keep it hot. Hot milk from the cows outside. Orange marmalade, and quince *mermelada* cut from a dense brick the color of dark amber, oranges from the trees below, eggs from the hens scratching under them, butter with a strong, rank taste and smell, from the same cows. Quitas bustled around the house putting things to rights, eventually coming to one of us to ask, "What more?" and then nodding, with a gesture that was part assent, part curtsey, and disappearing down the stairs. To me it seemed that she was a forest creature. I realized that I could not begin to imagine her life, when she was out of sight, or what was in her mind when she was there.

Antonio and Robertinho turned up at the door after breakfast to begin their studies. We had few books, to begin with, which would be another reason for a trip to Coimbra. We sat and made plans for organizing our mornings. Roberto was still so young that Dorothy said it made more sense for her to take care of his studies separately. For the moment, Anthony and I tried out a few of the books I had with me—some Scottish ballads, a Shakespeare, a Swift, translations of Homer—to see whether we could use any of them. He was wonderfully open and eager to listen, and to my amazement and delight, when I read him Shakespeare and the ballads slowly, he was caught up at once by them both. I gave him *Gulliver's Travels* to read on his own, and he read it in a few days, and reread it, and we talked about it as part of our lives. The same thing happened with Rieu's prose translations of *The Odyssey* and then *The Iliad,* and they supplied his reading for a while—though not for as long as I expected at first, for if I assigned him a chapter to read, or a book of one of the Homeric poems, he was likely to read two or three before he saw me next. I read Shakespeare to him every day, at the end of the morning studies—unless he had neglected to do his arithmetic assignment, or read his chapter of history (after we got books). If that happened he caught up on what he had missed in the time when I would otherwise have been reading him Shakespeare. He regarded his days without Shakespeare as punishment. He particularly loved Sir Toby Belch, Malvolio, the clowns in *A Midsummer Night's Dream,* and Falstaff, and wanted to hear their scenes over and over. He was a bright, excited, wide-eyed, quick child, and I felt that I was not teaching him so much as opening doors for him, leading him to subjects and writings that he then discovered for himself, and began to savor and possess. He knew more about some parts and some figures of Portuguese history than I did, of course, and I encouraged him to tell me about them, and then to learn more (when we had more books) so that he could tell me still more. (Peter had had some of the same love of reading, but he had liked to keep some of his treasured worlds, such as those of the sagas, somewhat to himself. Antonio seemed to talk without restraint about whatever excited him. His new enthusiasms were radiant, and it was a joy to watch him come to them.)

In the sitting room Dorothy initiated Roberto into the rudiments of addition and subtraction, quite painlessly, she said, and she read him Grimm's *Fairy Tales,* which we found when we went to Coimbra. He had just begun learning to read, and after she read the stories to him she let him read them slowly back to her.

I had the room off the sitting room inside the front door to work in, with a small table at the window where, when I looked up, I saw above the courtyard the porches with their white-washed beams and railings, and their strings of beans and peppers and onions drying in the morning sunlight, and the courtyard below, with its well, and the hens and ducks and geese coming and going. The house had taken us in without noticing that we were there.

32

We had been at the quinta only a day or two and were scarcely oriented to the surroundings, when Maria Antonia sent a message saying that she was going to Coimbra the next morning and inviting us along. Martin, her chauffeur, in his green livery jacket and peaked cap, was driving the big Buick when it pulled up outside the front door, next day after breakfast, and off we went, on a side road over the mountain. On the far side we followed the winding valley of the Mondego down to Coimbra. Martin parked in the open square facing the train station, near the river, and we all set out on foot from there, with shopping baskets.

The small inland city was another revelation. I had glimpsed a few bits of the industrial port of Genoa, and the narrow streets and back squares of old Nice, but Coimbra, with its small university founded in the thirteenth century, and its ancient church, the *Se Velha,* built like a fortress, was set firmly in medieval Lusitania, a palimpsest in which the Middle Ages and the nineteenth century showed through each other. The twentieth century, up until then, seemed to have brushed over it lightly. There were almost no cars, and a very few dilapidated trucks. A streetcar line led along the principal avenue, from the train station beside the river, up past the main cafés and the dimly lit stores, and snaked around up the hill to the upper squares, the *Se Velha* and the university. The sides of the streetcars were open when the weather favored it, and the students (all of them men) in their black gowns rode standing on the running boards, holding onto the brass poles between the seats and leaning out over the street, their robes flying like tiers of wings along the sides of the trolleys. The students never seemed to pay for their rides at all. The rest of the street traffic consisted of pedestrians, donkeys with packsaddles—sometimes a string of them, one behind the other—donkey carts, horse carts, a few bicycles. Everyone seemed to be in the habit of spitting, everywhere, all the time.

A succession of market squares ran parallel to the main street, down a flight of steps from it, and the cobbled spaces were filled with stalls and piled tables, and lined with artisans' shops. There were woodworkers of many kinds, makers of wooden bowls, toys, kitchen tools, pieces of furniture. There were weavers, behind hanging displays of blue and white bedspreads and tablecloths and curtains, made of crossed strands of flax and wool. There were coarse, shaggy blankets, undyed, and in stripes of the natural sheep shades of gray and tan and brown, or crossed with bands dyed bright red and green. Baskets of osier and bamboo in all sizes from dolls' handbags to donkey panniers, and huge hampers the size and shape of bass drums. Shoe- and boot-makers and repairers, cobblers at work sitting outdoors astride their three-legged benches. Toolmakers. Seed stores entrenched behind sacks. Vendors of fried cakes dusted with powdered sugar. Hatmakers. Rain cloaks. Musical instruments. Lanterns. Agricultural and gardening implements. Sharpeners, with grinding wheels the size of barrel hoops singing under blades. Barrels, kegs, and wooden buckets.

The bookstores had been installed in an earlier century, in which they were still rooted. Old ladders, worn shiny, rose into the upper shadows. My miserable, makeshift Portuguese, patched together, for the most part, from Spanish words, hopefully, hopelessly, was not a reliable help, but I found booksellers who knew some English, or Spanish, or French, and before long we had a real, two-volume Portuguese-English dictionary with a boiled-down Portuguese grammar in one of the volumes, and then I fell upon the Sa da Costa series of Portuguese classics, and the works of Gil Vicente, the *Cancionero da Ajuda,* a medieval *Crestomatia,* volumes of the nineteenth-century Portuguese novelists, and such oddities as Portuguese translations of Rilke and Pirandello. One store had schoolbooks for students of English, including graduated mathematics textbooks, and history books that would do for our morning lessons.

The farmers' market, on a series of tiers that descended to a magnificent fountain, was a cornucopia of piled fruits and vegetables and displays of the white cheeses and hard, Dutch-type cheeses of the region. I stood for a long time spellbound, watching one large, regal woman in a flowing head scarf and shawl, seated on the paving stones with the fountain behind her brilliant pyramids of oranges and tangerines. If a prospective customer paused in front of one of them and asked her about them, she would reach over to a pile, pick up an orange, cup it in both hands, and with a twist like a magician's gesture strip the skin from the upper half and hold out the opened fruit, lying in its skin as in a saucer, to be tasted. She was a figure of such grace and authority, sitting there with the fountain behind her, that I thought there must be legends about her.

The Mondego is wide in the valley there, with narrow islands in the middle, and the long bridge crossing to the south passed another great church, down in the river plain, a Gothic building, ancient but not as old as the *Se Velha.* It had been almost finished when the unprecedented weight of it had caused the water table below it to begin to give way, and slowly the whole elaborate edifice had sunk into the river, with the water filling it partway up the walls. There were places along the Coimbra side from which one could look across and see into the church, with the light from the unglazed Gothic window frames glinting on the water surface inside. Houses had been built against the outer walls like cliff dwellings, and a man with a boat could be hired to row one into the nave, and along the windows to the apse, where one could look back and see the reflection of the city, upside down on the dark water. His services were not sanctioned by the authorities, ecclesiastical or municipal. It was said that the roof was not safe, which probably was true. The government was in the process of expropriating and removing the buildings encrusted against the original walls, with a view to repairing the structure, but it was not going forward very fast.

We came back to Coimbra almost every week, and we all loved the town as it was then. Often we came with Maria Antonia in the Buick, and sometimes we took the small green train with the polished brass trim and the wood-burning locomotive that we had seen at the Serpins station. Again and again, as I walked on the cobbled, echoing back streets, it came over me with a rush that I was in *Europe,* in *Europe*—a fact as palpable as the donkeys and knife-sharpeners, as certain as my floundering dumbness in the language, but as hard to believe as though I had discovered that I was flying.

Once we came in to town when Maria Antonia's elder brother, Don Duarte, the "pretender" to the Portuguese throne, was visiting her. He had his own car, a mid-sized old Citroën, which he drove himself, and Maria Antonia had come with the Buick, and her chauffeur, Martin. Maria Antonia had invited us to have dinner over at the main house when Don Duarte and his wife had arrived, and I had liked him at once. He was a modest, quiet,

SUMMER DOORWAYS

well-read, witty man, who refused to take his position as seriously as those around him did, or at least that was the impression he gave. We had conversed easily from the beginning, and on that day when he and Maria Antonia had come to Coimbra together, each with appointments in the morning, the two cars had been parked outside a café across the square from the train station and left under Martin's eye, while we all went off into the town, agreeing to be back at a certain time. When Dorothy and I got back to the cars, Don Duarte was sitting at a café table having a late coffee and invited us to join him, and there we sat and waited for an hour, talking with him about his recent travels, and his rediscovery of Portugal, and how his sister had been late all her life, it was just one of those things. I listened to him, thinking of his own intricate, vexed, unresolved relation to everything around us, Coimbra, the people in the street, those who recognized him and those who did not, the entire country and its history. I tried to imagine what it might be like for him to explore the country at his age, seeing for the first time places and landscapes and houses that he had always heard about, but had come to see only when any claim to possession of them, which his family had believed in and some still did, no longer existed, and he had become, indeed, anyone, an outsider, hearing his own language with an outsider's ears. I thought of how improbable it was that I was sitting there with him laughing about his sister being late.

We grew fond of the green train that ran back and forth from Serpins to Coimbra, puffing calmly along the river valley, where the shallows appeared one by one around bends, and narrowed over rapids. On the way through the mountains the principal stop was at Louzá, a mountain town, its main street, at the foot of the hill, adorned with nineteenth-century facades and a small park enclosed by whitewashed balustrades. There were a few narrow streets leading up from there, and shops where dim naked bulbs glowed all day over piles of fabrics in the dark interiors. The stores sold bolts of woolen cloth, heavy shawls, blankets, a few rough, hand-knitted sweaters. There was a woodworker, and a cobbler with a window full of shoes waiting to walk out into 1900. A general store with fly-specked cans and jars on the shelves.

On the road above Louzá stood the ruins of a castle, built of a dark slatey stone laid horizontally, with no sign of mortar between the slabs. A great platform jutted out from the crag on which the walls clung above a deep gorge, with a stream splashing white, far below, and the remains of a watchtower and battlements rising around it. It became for me a distant but compelling image of Elsinore, the first scene of *Hamlet*, the sentries and the ghost; and the town, the train, arose in my mind, refracted, as models for scenes in *The Magic Mountain*, and Hans Castorp's life-and-death journey.

Louzá, tucked away in its valley, was metropolitan, a Babylon compared to Serpins, farther up in the mountains, with its one-story houses lining both sides of the unpaved yellow road, the doorways standing open, for about the length of a single city block. It felt like the end of the line, and it was. The locomotive sighed, and when we got off we walked along the quiet road, among the voices in the houses with their doors standing open, the sounds of pigs, chickens, and the soft splashing of the Ceira beyond them.

Two roads led up the valley from the village, one on each side of the river. The smaller of the two, a pair of ruts impassable to cars and used mostly by oxcarts and peasants with animals, swung wide around the level part of the valley with its patchwork of fields behind their low walls. A tiny shrine and chapel and two or three small houses that could not have had more than a single room in each of them were huddled in the middle of them. The dwellings did not have chimneys. Smoke seeped out between the roof tiles and drifted upward. The buildings, and the thin smoke, reflected whatever sunlight there was in the valley. Chickens glinted, scratching in the cabbage rows. The axle of an oxcart squealed away along the track.

The dirt road on the right, along the southeast side of the Ceira, was shorter and ran closer to the river. It was a mile or two to the quinta. Halfway along, a cluster of two or three buildings stood next to the road, stuccoed, with formal doorways. One of them was the schoolhouse for Serpins and the nearby mountain hamlets, and next to it was the house where the schoolmaster lived with his wife and their baby girl.

Maria Antonia had invited him to the main house to meet us, a few days after our arrival. I could see from his timidity that he and his wife had seldom, and probably never, been in the Comte's house before. The teacher was a quiet young man, from a provincial background, a small town somewhere as remote as Louzá, where his parents had a shop, and his position as a village schoolteacher was proof of his education. He had risen in the world. The nail of his little finger extended a full inch to show that he did no manual labor. He was small and thin, with a long, fine face, a gentle, kind man, and he was proud of knowing a little English. He was eager to help me learn Portuguese, and offered his services, with touching generosity. His wife was even more hesitant to say anything. She knew no English at all, and never seemed to utter anything more pronounced than a smiling murmur. He called at our front door a day or so after our meeting to invite us to his own house, where we sat in the dining room and had yellow cake and sweet wine. Then we went out for a stroll along the road, where he walked slowly with his hands clasped behind his back, and his wife followed with the baby in a stroller. He talked and I tried to follow what he was saying, and I had almost as much difficulty with his English as with his Portuguese. It was clear that he loved the region, which he had known all his life, and that he must know certain aspects of its history very well. I had questions about things I had seen there from the moment of our arrival—about the quinta, and the village. Maria Antonia had told me that a member of the Comte's family, perhaps his father, had kept his mistress in the house at the quinta, and I wondered whether the schoolmaster would ever talk about such scandalous matters, particularly when they involved people of title, members of a class above his own. Interested though I was in pursuing such possibilities, it took a burning effort for me to keep my attention on his mumbled, polite, hopeful syllables, his voice scarcely audible above the sound of our footsteps on the road, and as we strolled on at the deliberately meditative pace he preferred, I felt homesick for somewhere familiar, relatively native, thoughtless, and improbable in a way that I was used to.

We repeated the visit, with the same good intentions and helpless stiffness, at the quinta. Quitas brought us yellow cake too, for the occasion, and we poured wine, and *aguardente* in our black crockery coffee cups, and conversed like novices at chess, with tense pauses. After that we met on the road and went on with the slow stroll that was intended to distinguish us, I could see, from the steady, purposeful plodding of the men coming from the fields, or the flowing, barefoot grace of the women carrying heavy water jars balanced on coils of cloth on top of their heads. His pace, like his fingernail, signified his freedom from physical work, the higher level of his concerns, his serious leisure. His wife always walked behind, in peasant fashion, which made me uncomfortable. After a few of those awkward ambles she stayed in the house when we left, and Dorothy chose to stay at home too. Then he was likely to walk a bit more normally, and we would go into Serpins together, where he introduced me to friends of his, all of them men, of course, and artisans.

He took me to meet the maker of the tin lanterns, and I watched the man finish an elaborate one for hanging in the middle of a room. And to a cabinetmaker with a local reputation for his furniture, made to order. That man made tables and cabinets from fruitwood, and chairs of various kinds, but his real pride and pleasure was in making musical instruments. He had made guitars, violins, lutes, zithers, and he could play them all. The schoolmaster assured me that he was famous for miles around. His favorite instrument was the mandolin. He loved to make mandolins and to play them. At the schoolmaster's urging he picked up his own mandolin, one of his own making. It was ornate, the polished wood lustrous from long, loving attention. He tuned it for a moment, conspiring with it, and began to play, long tumbling arpeggios and complex chords, melodies floating through them. It sounded like an ancient music that perhaps had evolved in those mountains. Its sources could have been as distant as the music of the *Cancioneiro da Ajuda,* and before that, the *zagals,* the love songs of Moorish Spain. Passersby gathered outside on the road to listen, and the concert went on as the afternoon light deepened behind them.

As we walked back I told the schoolmaster that I would like to go there again and wondered whether that would be all right, and he assured me that it would. I took a bottle of wine the next time as a present, and the concert seemed even more elaborate. The schoolmaster asked me whether I would like to have a mandolin. I said I would, though I could not play it. The cabinetmaker, when he was told that, picked up a small, simple one, on a shelf by his head, that he said he had made that summer, and handed it to me. He was shy when I asked about the price. He said he wanted it to be a present, but I explained as well as I could that he was a professional artisan, and an artist, and should be rewarded for his work, and that I wanted to contribute to his art. He told me at last what he was used to receiving for a mandolin such as this one, and it seemed to me very little. The schoolmaster said that everyone in the valley who could play a mandolin had one from the cabinetmaker. I never learned to play mine.

The oxcarts wailed and moaned all day along the rutted track on the other side of the Ceira. Sometimes I, or we, walked into Serpins that way. Though it was longer, the view of the valley across the small fields, and the play of light, were more beautiful from over there. I learned that the tiny chapel in the middle of the valley was opened only for a few feast days every year, and for the weddings and funerals of peasant families living near it. It was so small that on these occasions only the priest and a handful of others could stand or kneel inside it. The rest gathered around the door, out in the day. I watched a procession approach it, one weekday morning, all in Sunday clothes, and assemble in a flock around the door.

The small house built against one wall of the chapel was the home of a woman of some education who worked for Maria Antonia as a housekeeper, and of her mother, a figure of unimaginable age whom I had seen out in the long honeyed light, feeding the chickens, and stooping in the cabbage plot. One day the younger woman saw us walking on the cart track and invited us in. The house was not as tiny inside as it appeared to be from a distance, but it consisted of a single room. The floor was of beaten earth, on ground level. The smoke that I saw rising through the roof tiles came from a small hearth against the chapel wall, which it had blackened up to the beams, and the beams too were black, and the undersides of the tiles. Drying flax was hanging in curtains, like laundry, across the room. There was a small field of flax outside the door, beyond the vegetable plot, and the woman we knew from the main house was proud of it. She said her mother still spun the flax, and she pointed to a distaff in the corner. She herself was attractive, but well past the age when most peasant girls were married. She had gone on in school longer than was usual around there and had wanted to be a schoolteacher. She said that Maria Antonia was going to help her continue her education.

When Maria Antonia's elder sister, Filippa, came to stay for a few days at the main house, both of them went to visit the small house built against the wall of the chapel. Filippa was shorter than Maria Antonia, gaunt and drawn and somewhat severe in manner, a director at heart, sharp, thin-lipped, and determined. She was concerned at once about the old woman, who in fact seemed quite content, happy with her house and garden and chickens. Filippa arranged for the daughter to take more food home from the main house. She wondered about how the old woman could keep warm when the winter came and the water froze. The daughter assured her that they had always managed, and were used to it. Most of all Filippa was worried about hygiene. Some aspects of it, she admitted, were better left unmentioned, but both she and Maria Antonia were startled when they found out that the old woman had never had a bath in her life. Filippa was aghast, and insisted that something must be done about it. The daughter was dubious, really opposed to the idea, but afraid to try to forbid it. That was the way her mother had grown up, she said, and it had done her no harm. She was old, indeed, but she was perfectly healthy. And her mother, when the idea of a bath was proposed to her, recoiled in horror. Maria Antonia and Filippa laughed about it, but Filippa said it was shocking, and that she had made up her mind.

Her daughter was very unhappy, but she believed she was helpless. Women from the main house, Quitas among them, carried a galvanized washtub and a pile of towels along to the lean-to house, and heated water in a circle of stone and ashes outside the door. I saw a procession of them heading along the cart track toward the chapel, but of course I did not see the rest.

When I had met the old woman she had not spoken at all but had smiled and nodded, and wandered away. I imagine that when Filippa and Maria Antonia approached her, and when she realized what they had in mind for her, she became rigid with refusal, her toothless jaw set, tears running down her face. Maria Antonia and Filippa no doubt tried to soothe her, telling her a lot of things that she did not understand or want to, and no doubt she turned her face away and stiffened as they began to unfasten her clothes, and felt humiliated but could not fight them off. They would have swathed her in towels and carried her like a white statue to the washtub in the middle of the floor, and stood her in the hot water, urged her to sit down in it, and then, whether she was standing or sitting, washed her all over.

She died of pneumonia within a week, and the next gathering I saw at the chapel was for her funeral.

33

For some reason women carrying water jars or baskets or basins of laundry on their heads seemed to meet on the road just above our front door and stand there, barefoot, carrying on long conversations in loud, high-pitched voices as though they were calling to each other from a distance, while turning slowly in place, around and back, under their burdens. In the days after the old woman's death they stood there longer than usual. I could not understand much of what I overheard through the door, but I knew they were talking about her.

Many afternoons Dorothy and I walked along the road, or the cart tracks into the mountains, or the footpaths, or simply went up the steep slopes under the stands of tall pitch pine trees that had been planted where the mixed forests had stood earlier in the century. Each of the pines had a blaze cut deep into the bark at waist level or lower, and a tapered terra-cotta bowl hanging under it to catch the pitch. The bowls were collected periodically and taken away to make turpentine. Arbutus bushes and wildflowers that may have been indigenous had survived the destruction of the original growth here and there. When we walked under the pines we took string bags and picked up big dried pinecones to burn in the fireplace, for the scent they gave the house.

The unpaved road by the front door of the farmhouse led on past walled fields between the road and the river. The fields were a few steps down from the road and were entered by stone gateways, carefully made, the steps worn with use. Beyond the fields, by the river, the tall, groaning wooden waterwheel, built by hand, was turned by the current in a channel that had been cut in from the river. It lifted the water from the Ceira into a narrow wooden flume at the edge of the field. The wooden cogs of the wheel reached out from the rim like paddles, turning it with its buckets, which filled one by one, and rose, spilling all the way, to empty at the top into the wooden flume made of hewn planks and held up on rows of stilts. The flume ran, leaking along its whole length, to the upper edge of the fields, where it poured out into an irrigation ditch. The whole system, powered by the river from which the water was drawn, played its complaining tune day and night.

The road climbed from the fields onto low bluffs, then to the edge of a small gorge through which the river came rushing over big rocks. At the top of the gorge, set back from the road along the cliff's edge, another chapel stood—one more local habitation of feminine divinity. The front door was always locked when we passed, but occasionally on Mondays there were trampled flowers and signs that the chapel had been frequented the day before. We looked through broken panes in the door into a small nave filled with sunlight, to the altar, and the small window in the apse above it. Some silent trust that had made the place was still living there.

Some days I took notebooks and books out onto a terrace under fruit trees, beside the house, and tried to write out there. A turkey from the barnyard below regarded my presence as an intrusion upon his domain, and he campaigned repeatedly to dislodge me. He strutted along the bottom terrace, three or four terraces below me, and delivered himself of lengthy, elaborate, inflated threats aimed in my direction. When I seemed to pay no attention to those, he stumped to the far end of the low terrace, out behind me, and flew up to the next one, a little nearer to me, and drummed along the whole length of it, back and forth several times, repeating his performance and imprecations. Still no result, so he made his way, behind me, up one more terrace, and then another, until he was on the same one where I was sitting, in an armchair, with a board and a book on my knees. From the end of the terrace in back of me he heaved himself forward squawking untranslatable battle cries. The first time it happened, I got up at that point and waved my arms in a little dance at him, and he unpeeled a woeful shout and heaved himself off the edge of the terrace to flap and flail all the way to the bottom, and start over again, in dudgeon. After that, rather than have to get up every time, I took an umbrella out with me, and when he began his final charge toward me along the terrace I raised it and opened it toward him, which sent him into his fit of consternation and flight. We played the game for days, apparently without change, but then he seemed to grow absentminded or acquiescent—I could not tell which—and days would pass without him coming to stalk me, until I began to miss him, and hope that he had not been undone once and for all. But as long as the warm days lasted, sooner or later he might turn up, catch sight of me from below, and unpack his exasperation, and we would go through our game, which had become a ritual for us both, something that he did not have to carry out more than once a day, to make his point, and assert his indignity.

I got to know the men who worked in the barns and storage sheds and orange grove and mill, and I tried hard to keep up conversations with them, to use the Portuguese words and phrases that I was memorizing from books and learning by listening. I was beginning to acquire a labored, floundering stick-drawing of the language. I was unreasonably impatient with it for not being Spanish—my first love—and impatient with myself because of that. But limited as it was, my grasp of textbook Portuguese permitted simple exchanges, which seemed like calling across a canyon, with the men on the farm. I could not tell how they were organized, how they were related, but they showed me the olive mill, opened the hatch door in the loud roaring lower room to reveal the ladder down into the millrace and the waterwheel turning, pointed out the gears carved on the heavy axle beams, slapped the piled round sacks for the olives, offered me their own harsh black wine, and laughed when nothing I said or asked made sense to them. Maria Antonia consoled me slightly by explaining that their Portuguese was not even the language I had been trying to learn, but a local, peasant variant of it—what is regularly referred to, in a distant, patronizing way, as a dialect—which she too found hard to understand some of the time.

There were still minstrels in the mountains, men who wandered, with musical instruments, a sack, and a shepherd's blanket. The quinta courtyard had been one of their stopping places, since some period in the past of which I knew nothing, a time that I hoped the schoolmaster or somebody might be able to tell me about. A singer, or several musicians, would appear in the barnyard, shouting an announcement, and then walk into the courtyard and stand by the well, knowing the place. The one who came most often was a tall, old, blind man with a beard, who put his hand on the rim of the well and stood looking upward. He had a large, beautiful zither, which he played with great delicacy, and sang songs of longing and mourning. Sometimes I did not see him arrive. At the sound of his playing I would rush to the window over the courtyard and look down to see his open mouth singing, and the song, the notes, the words were as impossible to grasp or retain as filaments of mist. Someone from the farm would bring him, or whatever musicians came and performed there, a jug of wine, slices of corn *broa* and white cheese, a tin plate piled with boiled potatoes and salt cod, *bacalao,* which the visitors would cut off in strips with pocketknives and manage to chew somehow, though there were not many teeth left among them. Quitas knew them all. She was not sure, at first, how we felt about them, and seemed a little embarrassed by them because we were there, but she stopped whatever she was doing to stand listening to them. She watched without expression as I took them money—my only way of thanking them and encouraging them to go on playing and singing and to return.

Something in my efforts to talk with the men on the farm must have got across to them, or encouraged their own curiosity, because one day several of those of my own age met me on the bridge and asked whether I would like to go with them that evening—it was a Friday—to a dance in one of the hamlets up in the mountains. I accepted at once. Should I bring Dorothy? They seemed dubious about that, and when I told her she said that she would rather stay home anyway, as she often did. The young men knocked at the front door after sunset, carrying lanterns. I lit one from the house, took a bottle of wine, and we left.

We crossed the river and went up along the ridge above the new house into the forest. The mixed growth had not been replaced by pines there. We climbed as the light faded around us under the trees. I could hear a stream splashing in a gorge below us. We stopped to light the lanterns, and walked on with the shadows dancing and leaping around us as though we were at sea, catching on black trunks and limbs, and waving on the path. Up on the mountain the night was turning cold. We walked for an hour or so. Then the trail dipped and turned and I saw lighted windows—soft lights, from lamps—and a partly open doorway, and heard music. Mandolins, an accordion or concertina, singing, the beat of dancing. Shadows crossed the light from the doorway. We walked down toward the house and found ourselves in a cluster of buildings in a hollow of the slope. At the house, my friends pushed the door open to a single room already crowded with young people of both sexes, most of them dancing to a fast beat, a whirling, high-stepping dance akin to a jig or a reel, which I would learn had variants in the mountain villages all the way across southern Europe. This was the first time I had seen it, but to those caught up in it in that room, so close together that every movement seemed to be transmitted through all the rest of them, out to the walls and back to the spinning dancers like a ripple on a pool, it was simply what dancing meant. The room was filled with the heat of bodies, the faces red and shining. They shouted and stamped with the beat. The floor and the walls shook. The jugs on the one sideboard shuddered and jingled, and the dance went on and on and suddenly stopped with a last stamping of feet.

Everyone was breathing hard, and there was a barny smell in the room. My friends who had brought me introduced me to another young man whose house it was, and that created a small, awkward hush around us as the others crowded closer to look at this stranger from somewhere that was only a name to them. I gave our host the bottle of wine, and he accepted it with a small formula of thanks, which I understood only in part, and then he offered me in turn a cupful of a sweet fortified wine—a variety of port. There seemed to be only a few cups, which were filled from a jug and passed around, and then someone stamped hard on the floor, a dance beat, and the instruments picked it up and the dance was off again.

Some of my companions joined in picking girls for partners, and in the next pause they began urging me to do the same. I protested that I did not know how, and they insisted that I should dance anyway. It was plain that they did not believe I did not know how to dance their dances. It was like saying that I did not know how to walk. All I had to do, they insisted, was to keep time. The beat began. One of the girls, a pretty one, was looking at me, and one of my companions gave me a little shove in her direction. I looked at her, questioning, and she nodded and we joined hands and I tried to keep time with the music, around and around the room, and managed to, more or less. The next dance was better. The step began to seem inevitable—an illusion caused simply by keeping in time with the music. As the dance after that one was announced with a stamp on the floor, my companion who had urged me to dance with my first partner tapped me on the shoulder and, with one of his friends, drew me outside the front door. There, with a remarkable awkward grace that I recognized despite the darkness and my poor grasp of the language, they explained to me that the young woman with whom I had been dancing was the *noiva* (the fiancée) of one of the men there, and that it was fine, and indeed an honor, for me to dance with her once. Twice was permissible. But more than that would not be right and might make for trouble. I apologized, but they said no, it was all right as it was, and we went back in and I was happy to stand watching for the rest of the time we were there.

The cups passed around between dances, and a few of the young men seemed to be showing the effects of it, but mostly it was the dancing itself that kindled the growing excitement in the room, which was in full fire when the young men I had come with suggested that perhaps it was time for us to start back. I thanked our host and we set out into the silence of the mountain path. After a bend or two we could hear the stream below us, then that sound was gone and we heard only our own footsteps. We had gone some distance when one of the men stopped suddenly, held up his hand for us to stop, put it over his mouth to signal to me to be quiet. I heard nothing, and then what sounded like quick breathing not far behind us. We stood listening. "Wolves," the first man whispered. He reached down to pick up a stone, and signaled for us to walk on. As we went he told me in whispers that it was common for them to have wolves follow them when they were up there on the trails at night. They would not bother us. They were harmless. They were simply curious. If they got too close all he had to do was toss a stone back in their direction, and they would be gone. We kept on walking. He walked behind the rest of us. At one point he flipped the stone back over his shoulder, paused a moment, and then paid no further attention.

The dances were always on Friday nights, and not every week. They would come by the quinta door in the afternoon and ask whether I would like to go with them, and we would start in the glow after sundown to walk for an hour or two across the mountains to another huddled flock of dark roofs, and the music and dancing, and once or twice more he put up his hand and said there were wolves behind us. I have never known whether it was a game they meant to play on the foreigner, or whether there really were wolves following us on those trails at night.

34

On the far side of the Ceira a cart track followed the rising bank upstream and wound on into the woods. Footpaths led off it. The only way to find out where they led was to follow them, and Dorothy and I did that, or sometimes I went alone, all the way to some remote building, perhaps a goatherd's hut, or to where the track vanished in a stand of forest. We followed the cart road across the river farther and farther, one day starting earlier than usual. We came to a long rise, as though we were climbing out of the upper end of the valley. There were woods above us, a grove of mimosas. At a bend of the track there was a house standing by itself. It was not a peasant dwelling but a two-story structure, with chimneys at both ends, and long windows. When we got up to it we could see that it was set back from the road, on the edge of the rise, with a view far down the valley behind us, which we had begun to know, and over the ridge in the opposite direction into another valley that was full of shadow. The house looked bare but not neglected. Someone must have been taking care of it regularly. And as we stood in front of it we saw at the same time the way we had come, full of the long, late afternoon light, and the other valley and its shadow, reflected in the windows. I supposed that it must be the summer house of some family in Coimbra, or even farther away, who perhaps had just left it to go back to town after the season. I asked Maria Antonia whom it belonged to, but she told me she did not know.

Summer lasted late along the small valley. It was summer light that lingered in honeyed beams through the afternoons, over the small fields, and lit up the cart track across the river, the bronze hides of the oxen, the mud-caked cart wheels turning slowly and wailing, the wisps of mauve smoke climbing. But the nights were growing colder in the shadowed courtyard, and the house was cold in the mornings. The water in the hens' drinking basin had ice on it at daybreak. Quitas left a fire laid in the bathroom wood-stove, and I lit it first thing, before she came up the stairs with breakfast. By late morning the summer seemed to be back again, the season in which we had come, yet in my room over the court-yard the sun never shone, and I worked with one of the shaggy blankets over my legs.

When Maria Antonia told us, before Christmas, that the Comte de Feijo had offered her his villa in Estoril, on the estuary west of Lisbon, and that she was planning to move there for the rest of the winter, it came as a blow to me. I had come to love the quinta. I was captivated by my glimpses of the life around it. Dorothy seemed to have settled happily into the quiet days there.

I asked Maria Antonia whether we would come back later, and she could not say, and I was not sure whether she wanted to. She liked it, she said, but it was not really practical, for long. That sounded like something I had been unhappy to hear in my childhood.

So we would move out of the farmhouse to Estoril, and a villa next door to the one belonging to the exiled King of Spain, and there Anthony would meet Juanito, who would one day be the King, and we would all play kick the can in the walled garden, and Dorothy and I would sit in the same small movie house with King Mark of Rumania and Umberto of Italy, both of whom lived nearby. We would have an apartment above the carriage house and stable, and I would go riding with the Comte's head groom, up over the mountain to Sintra and its palace on the other side. We would explore Lisbon, and travel across Spain on milk trains, and I would visit Robert Graves on Mallorca, who would turn out to need a tutor for his son and would offer me the job.

And indeed I would not go back to the Quinta Maria Mendes ever again, or learn more about it, or see the schoolmaster or the cabinetmaker or Quitas or the blind singer or any of the faces there. I would not go back to St. Jean Cap-Ferrat, either, and would not see Josephine or the Frataccis. I would not see Alan again. Effie Halsey told me on the telephone that Alan had died, around the time of our move to Estoril, when he was on the ship coming back from Europe. He fell down a companionway and struck his head. I would not see Alain Prévost either. After we lost touch, that last winter at Princeton, I tried to find an address for him in France, imagining that he must be somewhere around Paris, but by the time I managed to trace him, through Ralph Woodward, a former roommate of his, Alain had died several years earlier, suddenly, of a heart attack, on his farm in Normandy, when he was forty-one years old. He had written six novels by then, one of them based on a summer at Princeton. I never saw his sister, Françoise, again either. By the time I learned what had happened to Alain, she too was dead.

But when we left the quinta I had seen something that I was to come to in various forms before I was old enough to be able to look back and recognize it. The move away from the valley of the Ceira would lead through years in which, again and again, I would have the luck to discover, to glimpse, to touch for a moment, some ancient, measureless way of living, of being in the world, some fabric long taken for granted, never finished yet complete, at once fixed as though it would never change, and evanescent as a work of art, an entire age just before it was gone, like a summer.